Last Chance Texaco

Last Chance Texaco

CHRISTINE POUNTNEY

faber and faber

First published in 2000
by Faber and Faber Limited
3 Queen Square London WC1N 3AU

Typeset by Faber and Faber Ltd
Printed in England by Clays Ltd, St Ives plc

A CIP record for this book
is available from the British Library

ISBN 0–571–20144–X

2 4 6 8 10 9 7 5 3 1

One day my mother let a bum into the house. He rang the doorbell and asked for money. My mother took pity on him and let him in. She gave him a bowl of her homemade soup and thick slices of fresh bread still steaming with little square pads of butter melting in the centre. When he had finished, she let him have a shower, lent him my dad's bathrobe and even gave him a shirt and a pair of pants that my dad never wore anymore. When the man emerged from the bathroom, he looked completely different. I was eight years old, but even I could tell he was very handsome.

He was an Indian from the reservation, just outside of Bella Coola off the coast of British Columbia. He was tall and muscular. He had a noble face and strong nose like an arrowhead. His skin was flawless. His hair was like ink pouring down his back. When he came back into the kitchen, he sat down again and my mother placed a cup of coffee in his hand. She sat across from him and took one of his cigarettes. I sat at the end of the table with my chin resting in the small bowl of my fists.

He stayed all afternoon and told stories that made my mother laugh. She poured him cup after cup of coffee. The ashtray gradually filled up. She got up and emptied it into the garbage. I left and went to play in my room. When it started to get dark, I returned to the kitchen. My mother was leaning across the table and had her hand on his. She was saying something soothing like she was consoling him. When she saw me come in, she gave his hand a quick squeeze then got up and started busying herself at the counter. She made a couple of sandwiches. She put a few bottles of beer into a plastic bag, some fruit and the sandwiches. Then she left the room.

I looked up at the Indian. He stared back at me from his chair. He raised one arm and reached behind his back. He drew an invisible arrow from a quiver and slotted the groove into the string of his bow. He pulled the string back as far as it would go, straining the wood. He released his fingers and let the arrow fly. It hit me full in the chest. I felt the thunk of metal and stumbled backwards. He laughed. He got out of his chair and walked over to me and tousled my hair. He lifted me up and swung me around the room.

Little fella soars like a bird, he laughed as I careened through the air.

My mother came back into the kitchen and the Indian put me down. She walked over to the counter and slipped an envelope into the plastic bag. She handed him the bag and said, You'd better hurry up. He followed her to the door.

Two weeks later, my mother ran away. I never saw her again. I came home from school to an empty house. The lights were on and there was a bowl of cold soup on the table and a peanut butter sandwich. On the top slice lay the torn-off corner of a page of looseleaf. She had drawn a heart in black pen and coloured it in with red Magic Marker. I put the heart inside my sandwich face down on the peanut butter and squeezed it shut. I ate the soup first and then I polished off the sandwich. I even ate my crusts.

After my mom left, my dad started drinking and getting into fights. He'd come home in the middle of the night. His face started to change. His eyes lost their sheen, like pebbles on the beach that are brilliant underwater but go grey and matt when you bring them home. His mouth grew tight and wiry like a coil or a spring, ready to shoot off at any minute. He lost his job at the cannery. He was forced to borrow money.

He spent a lot of time in front of the TV. He'd sit on the sofa with a bottle of beer in one hand and a cigarette in the other. His face was expressionless. He looked exhausted. I'd watch the ash of his cigarette burn down to the filter. He never cooked. I made myself toast. I ate tuna straight out of the can.

One night as I lay awake in my bed there was a loud banging at the door. I heard men's voices and the door slam. A man said, Okay, Orin. It's time to pay up.

I have a son to think about, my dad pleaded in a voice I hardly recognized.

There was a scuffle and a chair fell backwards. I heard a few muffled thuds and a whimper. Something exploded like a fuse-box and glass shattering. I slid off my bed and crept underneath. I stared at the crack of light under my door. The men left. I pulled my knees up to my chest.

I didn't move until morning when all the shadows in my room were gone and daylight had made it safe. I tried to stand but my legs were cramped with cold. I rubbed my thighs and sat down on my bed. When I felt strong enough, I went out to the hall and walked into the livingroom. My dad lay curled up on his side by the TV. The whole screen was smashed. I looked down at his face. There was a lump like a dough-ball where his eye should have been.

Are you okay? I asked.

He groaned.

Should I call an ambulance?

He rolled onto his back and grabbed my ankle. He held it very tight for a couple of minutes. When he released it, I went into the kitchen and poured myself a glass of water. I made my dad a cup of coffee. I put a cigarette in his mouth and lit a match. My hands were steady but my heart trembled.

We left that afternoon. My dad put all our clothes into three big garbage bags and threw them into the back seat. He packed two pillows and our sleeping bags, some records and his shaving kit. He took a photo album from his dresser. I walked into my room and pulled a blank. I wanted to take everything but my dad had told me, Only take what you can't replace.

I left my felt pens and my colouring books. I left my teddy bear. I left my rock collection and my plastic tomahawk with the fake feathers. As I was leaving my room, I unhooked my mask and snorkel from the doorknob and put them on. We backed out of the drive and I watched the house recede in the oval frame of my mask. I turned around and hung my arms over the back of the front seat. I watched as my street disappeared behind the fogged-up glass of my deep-sea diving mask. I listened to the rise and fall of my own hot breath. Drool collected in the bend of my snorkel. We drove south out of Bella Coola for the very last time.

After a couple of hours, we stopped at a drive-in and ate

hamburgers and fries. I spilt ketchup on the seat and looked up at my dad expecting to be told off. He looked indifferently at the red smudge on the brown upholstery, then continued to stare out the front windshield. He took another bite of his hamburger and winced. Maybe it was the pain in his jaw that was preoccupying him, but he didn't say anything for the whole next leg of the journey. We kept heading south until we hit the American border. We slowed down and glided up to the border station. My dad turned to me and said, Take that thing off. I peeled off my mask and pulled the warm, wet snorkel out of my mouth. It smelt like grease and ketchup. My dad leaned out the window and exchanged a few words with the man in the booth.

Fishing trip, my dad answered. It's a holiday.

Looks like you need one, the border guard said. Hope they're biting, he called and waved us on.

Five miles down the road, my dad pulled over on the side of the highway. He reached across me and pulled his passport out of the glove compartment. He leaned back in his seat and flipped through the blank pages. Then he tore it up. He wound his window down and watched the little shreds of paper float to the ground.

We're starting over, he said, then spun the tires on the gravel and took off. It was spring and the wind blew in cool. I tucked my scarf into my collar and hunkered down for the long haul. I had no idea where we were headed. I don't think my dad did either. I looked back down the highway. In the wake of a semi, I saw the small white petals of my dad's passport rise and scatter across the road.

*

Two months later we settled down in a little shack surrounded by pine trees on the edge of a small town called Round Bay, on the coast of California. My dad committed welfare fraud and we lived off his meagre allowance. He enrolled me in the local school and lied about our papers.

It took me a whole year to get used to the idea that we weren't going back to Bella Coola. My dad had made up his mind. He didn't want to talk about it. And anyway, how do you explain to an eight-year-old that his life has changed for good? I kept expecting my mother to walk through the door hugging a bag of groceries, saying she was sorry it'd taken her so long. She'd put away the groceries and start mixing the ingredients for bread, rolling the dough out onto the table and punching it down like I'd seen her do a hundred times before.

But she never did come through the door and eventually I stopped expecting the smell of freshly baked bread to greet me when I got home from school. Instead, I got used to the sour smell of booze and cigarettes, dishes that needed doing and sheets that needed washing.

One night, after I'd taken off my dad's shoes and was pulling the covers over him like I did whenever he passed out on his bed fully clothed, I saw a photograph sticking out of his breast pocket. I took it to my bedroom and shut the door. I got in under the blankets and turned on the flashlight and stared at it for a very long time.

It was taken on an angle as if it had been taken in a hurry, in a garden with lots of people, like they were having a barbecue. It must have been nearly dark because the lights from the house in the background were white against the dark grey outline of trees to either side. I recognized my father to the left of the photo although the top half of his head was cut off. He was grinning but since I couldn't see his eyes there was no telling what that smile meant. He was holding a woman up by the arm. His fingers dug into her flesh. She was small and must have been very light. Her body was twisted slightly away from the camera like she was off-balance. It was hard to tell if he was pulling her up off the grass or keeping her from falling over. All I could see was the outline of her cheek, but I knew it was a picture of my mother.

I wanted to talk to her. I wanted to know where she was. I wanted to know if she remembered me, if she ever thought about me. I wanted to see her face because I was forgetting what she looked like.

I wonder if it worked out with the Indian.

Something nice my father did for me was to let me keep that picture. Either that or he forgot he had it. Maybe he thought he'd lost it. Maybe he didn't give a shit. At any rate, I cut him out of the photograph and pasted my mother's twisted frame to the bottom of a wooden cigar box where I kept my treasures: a silver sand dollar, two toy soldiers, a cuff-link I found on the beach one day. Things that found their way into my pockets.

Part One

You're gonna kill yourself one day, my father said when he saw me standing in the kitchen with a towel slung over my shoulder.

Naw. Not in the water, I said. You might, but I'd never. I can't drown. I'm a fish, I added, taking the milk from the fridge and drinking straight from the carton.

You're crazy is what you are.

No, I'm not.

Just don't expect any sympathy from me when you break your neck.

I won't, I said, standing in the cool light of the fridge watching the steam roll out like spirits round my feet.

And get me a beer seeing as you've been staring into the fridge for the last twenty minutes.

Get it yourself.

Don't give me any lip, John.

So don't call me crazy, I mumbled, placing a King Can on the arm of the livingroom sofa.

I'll call you what I like. Now beat it.

I am, I said and walked over to the door and shoved my feet into my sneakers.

I left the house and walked through the pine trees sloping up towards the bluffs. I knew the way by heart, which was good because it was very dark. A thin quarter-moon sliced through the upper branches and stars flicked on and off like city lights. The forest creaked with nighttime.

When I got to the point, I stripped down to my shorts and stretched my arms over my head and behind my back. I felt the tug and pressure of muscle, then a rush of blood. I walked to the edge of the cliff and looked out at the ocean, black and shiny as an oil slick, its surface unbroken by whitecaps. I could hear the waves sighing twenty feet below, moving in then pulling back, carving ancient signatures into the rock.

I bent my knees and stood poised, ready as a slingshot. I closed my eyes and listened to a wave shudder the coast and the after-hiss as it dragged itself out again. Another wave toppled and rumbled like thunder. It dissolved into a white froth. I waited for the next one to atomize and launched myself into the spray. I heard the wind in my ears just before I hit the water. Cold rushed into my armpits. My balls seized up. Everything went soundless and dark. I plummeted until the buoyancy of my lungs began to slow me down and pull me up. I arched my back and scissored my way to the top and broke the surface of the water, panting for breath.

I got up the next day and rode into town on my bicycle. The road was dry and dust settled on my running shoes like gunpowder. I stopped pedalling and coasted down the hill towards the beach. The beach was the length of a football field only shaped like a new moon lying on its side. The sand was light brown and sparkled in the sunlight like crushed glass. The beach dropped steeply so the water didn't go out much at low tide. The steep drop created a serious undertow and swimmers were warned to be careful. I looked out at the ocean as I cycled past and it winked back at me.

Town was another five minutes by bike. It took longer to get to than ride through. There was a main street with a few stores and four parallel rows of residential blocks to either side, as orderly as graph paper. Someone had installed a lone set of traffic lights at the intersection between Main and Alta Way, which was the street you took from the highway into town, but apart from that there weren't many other indications to suggest that it was 1985. The turn-off was easy to miss, not even a signpost near the exit, so people who'd never been to Round Bay probably didn't even know it existed. I propped my bicycle up outside Shirley's Diner and walked in.

Shirley's place was like home to me. She'd caught on pretty early that I was the kind of kid that needed a bit of looking after since nobody else was gonna do it, so she often let me eat for free and always had advice on hand. There were six booths down the left-hand side and a long Formica counter on the right with six vinyl-covered stools. The fourth one was cracked and taped and pinched the skin on the back of my thighs. I only ever sat on that one if all the other ones were taken. The walls were covered in red and black felt wallpaper, like something left over from an old frontier brothel or saloon, but this was not a saloon. Shirley didn't like loitering so she never served alcohol and let the singles warp in their jukeboxes and never bothered replacing them. Sometimes the radio would be on with the baseball game or the golden oldies.

On the wall behind the counter was a large mirror. It had wire-thin, copper-coloured fissures painted on it so that it looked like marble. The first thing I always saw when I swung the door open Clint Eastwood-style and the little bell wagged on its hook was the back of Shirley's bleach-blonde head reflected in the mirror. Shirley was overweight and in her fifties and had been running the place ever since my dad and I arrived in Round Bay. She always wore the same blue apron with white trim and her name stitched in cursive across her right breast.

The place was just winding down after the breakfast rush. Shirley took one look at me and clucked her tongue. Sit down, she said and eyeballed me onto a stool and I'm glad to say it wasn't the fourth one because I had on a pair of cutoffs that day.

Your father came in here yesterday.

I didn't think he ever left the house.

Ya, well he came round yesterday.

So?

Well, he was trying to sell Mick a bicycle.

Where the fuck's he gonna get a bicycle from?

Watch your mouth, kid.

He doesn't own one.

He wants to trade yours.

He can't have my bike!

Asked Mick if he'd take it in exchange for some credit at the store.

What the fuck's Mick gonna do with my bicycle?

Mick's got a kid, you know.

Mick's got a *girl*.

Well anyways, your dad came in here asking all the usual questions. Why he never sees you hanging out with anybody else. Why you don't seem to have any friends, that sort of thing.

And what did you tell him?

I told him you were queer.

Oh thanks, Shirley.

Aw, come on. Don't pay any attention to him.

I don't, I said and stared a hole in the counter top. I just don't understand why he can't mind his own business, that's all.

He hasn't got anything better to do. He's bored.

Well, I'm not.

And the fact is, John, he cares a lot more about you than he lets on.

Well, he's got a funny way of showing it.

It's not easy for men. They have a hard time showing their feelings.

Ya, well that's not my problem.

Oh, don't give me that tough-guy act.

Fine, but it doesn't mean I have to care about what he thinks of me. I mean, what has he ever done for me?

Well, he's raised you, hasn't he?

If that's what you wanna call it.

Look, he just wants to know that you've turned out okay. He wants you to be normal.

What, like everybody else around here?

He wants you to be happy.

And hanging out with those idiots is gonna make me happy?

But they're your friends, John.

They're idiots.

Well, they're the only idiots you've got to hang out with.

I'd rather hang by myself.

[17]

Suit yourself, but it's not gonna help to ease your father's mind. He doesn't see the difference. He expects you to be just like the rest of them.

But I'm not.

I know that.

It's not my fault.

I'm not saying it is, she said, wiping her hands on her apron. God, that dog out there's been barkin' all morning.

Whose is it?

I don't know, but I wish someone would put it out of its misery. You hungry? Had any breakfast? How 'bout some waffles?

Shirley went into the kitchen. When she came out, she said to me, What you need is a girl.

What I need is a boat, I replied. I got an idea for a business, Shirley. Scuba-diving. I could fetch things down there. It's beautiful. Abalone, coral, starfish. I could take the tourists out. Get the gear. A license.

We don't get any tourists, John. Town's too small for that.

But we're so close to Santa Barbara. All those resorts? We're not far from LA, either.

Ya, but this town ain't much to look at, if you know what I mean.

Halfway through her sentence someone leaned on a car horn outside and held it down. That horn kept blasting and blasting. That dog barking and barking. Making a racket and disrupting everybody. Jesus Christ.

Shirley stopped fussing with the glasses she was drying and rolled her eyes at me. We waited but the noise wouldn't stop.

Aw, shut the fuck up, one customer muttered.

People in the diner began to lift themselves out of their chairs to peer into the street. Two old men with hats standing outside the window pointed at something and shook their heads. Shirley slapped her dishtowel onto the counter and nodded to me.

Let's go see what this is all about.

She swung the door open, making the curtains swish. I followed her out onto the sidewalk and we headed towards an old blue Chevy pick-up truck where the honking was coming from. It said *Foxy's Fresh Seafood Daily* in crooked letters across the side. The sun was glaring off the windshield and we had to get pretty close to see into the cab. When we were close enough, we saw that there in the driver's seat sat a dog with its paw up on the horn, barking like a general, creating havoc all down Main Street.

Shirley laughed and smacked the window. The dog bounded to the other side, the honking stopped, and the dog stuck its tongue out the window.

I was just leaving Mick's Greengrocers, with a stolen green apple and a brand new *Super Heroes* comic book rolled up in my back pocket, when Ben called me from across the street. He jogged over.

Hey, ya old shit! Where the fuck you been?

Here.

I mean I've been looking for you since school got out. Where ya been?

Here. The beach.

I been to the beach every afternoon for the last two weeks.

I don't go in the afternoon.

Well, ya missed a show. Babe got drunk on Saturday and this time everybody got to see her tits.

Sorry I missed it, I said.

Man, I've been beating off to those tits for years.

Everybody has. What happened?

Well, the guys told her Mr Brodsky was going to be at the beach, you know, the new English teacher every girl is gaga over? So she came down in a bikini. Can you believe it? Holy fuck! You should've seen her. Out to here! Nothing holding her back. So we kept giving her beer and after she'd had like almost a whole six pack, Derrick goes up to her from behind and unclips her bikini top and runs off with it. She was too drunk to chase him, sort of just stumbled after him, you know? We were killing ourselves laughing. But I bet you every guy there had a fucken hard-on. Hey! You listening to me or what?

Ya, ya, I said and looked up towards the sun so that the tops of the telephone poles along the edge of the street disappeared into a blur of light. The light was burning patterns of telephone poles onto my retina, I could tell. I could feel the hollow balls of my eyes heating up. I forced myself to keep staring until my eyes began to water and blink uncontrollably. I squinted and then out of the haze emerged the figure of a girl. Thick-set and strong-looking. Black hair cut short around her square face and lips the colour of pomegranate seeds. She was wearing a black halter-top and blue shorts. She walked right up to me and past me, looked at me quickly and said, Hi. I immediately got this mentholated feeling in my chest, like when you rub Vicks VapoRub on it then breathe in vigorously.

Ben swivelled on his heels and let out a whistle. She's the new girl, he said. Just moved here with her father. Got some weird last name.

What's her name? I asked, still staring in the direction she had come from.

I dunno. Hey! Snap out of it.

Ben shoved me, then punched me square in the shoulder which made me close my mouth.

Aw, forget it, he said. You're fucken hopeless.

I spent all afternoon thinking about the new girl. I needed some way to impress her. She was beautiful and I had nothing. I decided to go see Peter, so I headed down to his clapboard boathouse on the beach.

Hey there, John, he said from the other side of a knotted fishing net that he was checking for tears. Haven't seen you in a while.

I been around.

I know you have. Just haven't seen you, that's all.

How's the fishing?

Not too bad.

Got any work?

What kind of work?

Any kind.

You need some cash, son?

I wanna buy a boat.

A boat, huh?

Yep.

What kinda boat? A schooner? Ketch? Trawler? Just what kind of boat you aiming to buy there, Johnny-boy?

I know a bit about boats. I'm not claiming to be an expert, but I'm not as naïve as all that. I understand the water.

You understand the water, huh? So tell me, how much have you learned in all your years?

I know its power 'cause I've felt it. I respect the ocean. It needs to be honoured.

Honoured? I'm sure it'd be pleased to hear that. But honour's a bit lofty a sentiment, don't you think? You can't just go out on the water without having any technique. What if something happened? What if you capsized? What if there was an emergency? Do you know the signal for danger? For help? You have to know about tides and currents, weather systems and coastal lights. You wanna have flares on board and lamps so the other boats can see you. You have to learn to navigate and read maps. What if you got caught in a squall? There are offshore drifts that'd carry you clear to Mexico before you had the chance to say Jack Daniels, and then what?

There was an awkward pause. I shuffled the sand between my toes. Peter looked embarrassed and fidgeted with the net.

A rowboat, I said quietly. Just a fucken rowboat . . .

I got a rowboat out back needs scraping and a paint job. It'll take you a while to do but in return you can have Lil, the one that's upturned. Still needs a lot of work, but she's yours today if you start on the other one this week, how's that?

I smiled and shook Peter's hand, Thanks, man. And something slow and lifeless in me slid off like a snake's skin and something hopeful and energetic remained in its place. I ran back behind the shed and righted my boat. Lil. The gunnel was cracked. The bench was rotting in the middle and eaten away by termites. I was overjoyed. I made a mental list of things to do.

I had a boat. I had a chance to get the girl.

I was cycling down Main Street the next time I saw her. She was heading into Mick's so I skidded to a halt, jumped off my bike and charged inside. The transition into darkness blinded me and I nearly bumped into her at the counter.

Hi, Mick. Gimme some razors. And four of those Jaw Breakers, I said out of breath, fumbling in my pocket for some change.

Three sixty-five, John. What's the matter with you today?

Three? I whined, fishing around in my other pocket. Um ...

Want me to put it on your dad's tab?

No. Just forget the razors. Here's a buck for the Jaw Breakers. Aw Christ, I swore as I dropped the small paper bag and two electric-blue balls rolled across the counter and onto the floor. I didn't bother picking them up. Just ran for the door not daring to look back.

Gotta be puberty, Mick sighed. Helluvan awkward age.

Out in the sunlight, I broke into a fresh sweat. I picked up my bicycle where it had landed and swung my leg clumsily over the seat, stumbled a few paces and crushed a testicle between the crossbar and my thigh. Doubled over in pain, I peddled off towards Shirley's.

I limped into the diner and sat down sideways on the edge of a stool and placed my greasy little bag with the two remaining Jaw Breakers on the plate in front of me. The sight of those things nearly made me cry and I was about to tell Shirley to forget my lunch 'cause I had no appetite when the door swung open and the girl walked in. I felt myself go red and quickly swivelled round, knocking a goddamn fork to the floor.

Shirley took one look at the girl and said, Wanna milkshake?

Do you have any cake? the girl asked.

No, but we have pie. Apple or cherry. Best in town, isn't that right, John? She turned to me and finished me off with a wink.

Cut it out, Shirley, I thought to myself. I'm dying here. I'm absolutely dying. Help me, for chrissake.

Mind if I sit here? the girl asked.

Mind? I screamed. Hell no. Free world, ain't it? Then bowed my head and tried as best I could to hide behind my hair.

I'll bring you each a piece, Shirley said to the top of my head. Apple or cherry?

I found the question embarrassing. Um . . . apple for me, I mumbled.

Me too, said the girl.

Two apple it is then.

The pie came and we ate it and neither of us said a word. Simultaneously we both got up to go.

How much do I owe you? the girl asked.

It's on the house this time, Shirley said with mischief in her eyes.

As we were leaving, she pulled me aside and said, Say something for godssake. And don't be so nervous.

The girl turned and looked me square in the face while she pulled the door open. After you, she said.

Once outside, we kicked dust up on the sidewalk and I

thought this girl must be tough or something. Sticks her hip out way too far when she's just standing around. She's got all these bruises on her body and Band-Aids on both knees. I sat down on the curb to contemplate. The girl also sat down, took a cigarette from a pack in her pocket and lit up a smoke.

You shouldn't smoke, I said. It's bad for your lungs.

Aw fuck off, she said.

I can't smoke. I'm not supposed to.

Why? You sick or somethin'?

No.

Then how come?

'Cause I'm a diver. I need all my lung capacity. I can hold my breath up to two, three minutes underwater.

Bullshit.

It's true.

No, you can't. That's impossible.

I'll show ya.

What, right now?

Down at the beach.

I guess, she said, and brushed her ass off and put the cigarette out with the toe of her sneaker and tucked a stray wisp of hair behind the prettiest little ear, like a rose bud with tiny little leaves and soft rubbery thorns that hadn't grown brittle yet.

I picked up my bike and we headed for the beach.

So where you from? I asked.

Boston.

That's far, isn't it?

Kinda. Not if you fly. It only took us five hours.

What brought you here?

My dad. Wanted a quiet place to work. It's cheap here, too.

[25]

And nobody's ever heard of it before. Nobody knows this place even exists. It's like cut off from the outside world.

What does he do?

He's a writer.

And your mom?

How come you ask so many fucken questions?

Sorry. Ask me one.

How old are you?

I'm seventeen, I said.

Bullshit.

Sixteen.

No, you're not.

I'm fifteen, okay? I'm fucken fifteen.

Are you really?

Yes, I said. And you?

I'm sixteen, but I'll be seventeen in December . . . You're not a very good liar.

She was a whole year older than me. One year older and the most beautiful woman I'd ever laid my sorry eyes on in all my life.

I own a boat, I said. Wanna see it?

Maybe later. I don't know how to swim.

Doesn't know how to swim? She doesn't know how to swim? I was still shaking my head in disbelief when we came to the path that led up to Adam's Point. That was like not knowing how to eat, not being able to fall asleep.

Where are we going? she asked me, slightly out of breath, as the path ended and the rocks rose steeply into the air.

I want to teach you how to swim, is what I had in mind but

all I said was that we were gonna climb these rocks and I was gonna dive off the top and she could count the minutes before I surfaced. I took off my high tops and my t-shirt and turned to face her in my cutoffs. She stood there with her hands on her hips, chewing gum the way some kids kick tin cans.

No way, she said.

Whaddya mean?

There's no way I'm going up there.

How come?

Don't wanna.

I know a way. It's perfectly safe.

I'm not scared. I just don't wanna climb all the way to the top.

But you won't be able to see me dive from down here.

What's the big fucken deal?

I thought you wanted to see how long I could stay under-water.

What's it to you?

I want to prove to you that I can hold my breath for as long as I said.

Well?

Well, I'm gonna do it anyway. I'll give you enough time to get down to the beach, then I'll dive and swim around the point to where you can see me. I'll stay underwater the whole time.

And I'm supposed to believe that you haven't come up for air, not once?

Ya.

Whatever.

I'm not a good liar, remember?

Fine, she said and cracked her gum like a mouthful of caps, then turned and strode through the sand grass down to the water.

After scrambling over the first few rocks at the base of the cliff, I turned and yelled, Hey! What's your name? I don't even know your name!

Without looking back or breaking her stride, she called out, Anna Arvanitakis!

Nice to meet you, Anna! I'm John! John Wade!

I turned and grabbed on to a jagged boulder and squeezed my body through a gap in the rocks. After that, they were like steps and easy to climb. At the top, I stood for a moment and breathed the salty air in deeply through my nose. I looked at the coast to my left and the surf in the distance and thought about Anna standing on the beach, shielding her eyes from the glare of the sun, staring out at the point and waiting for me to appear. I walked to the edge and studied the swell of the water below, rising like cake batter over the rocks then shrinking back down again. I wiped my sweaty palms on the back of my shorts, sucked in a lungful of air and dove off the edge. I hit the water like an arrow shot from Cupid's bow and the cold, dark mouth of the ocean swallowed me up.

I ran out of breath and surfaced, swam out to sea and hung on my back to catch my breath. I watched a seagull circle on a hot air stream. I still wanted to impress her so I dove again and swam like a frog around the point. When I came up for air, I could see her standing on the shore looking out at me. I waved to her from the water and she casually raised a hand back at me.

Well? I asked, when I'd swum up to meet her.

Well what?

How many minutes do you think that was?

I dunno. I wasn't counting. Besides, how the fuck was I supposed to know when to begin? It's not like I could see you or anything.

True, I said.

You swam the whole way underwater? she asked, pulling at the hem of her shorts and tilting her head sideways.

Almost. I had to come up for air once. I was too impatient. The trick is to stay calm. Move as slowly as possible. You want to conserve energy, use the water to your advantage. Try to make your body streamline.

And where d'ya learn that?

I did a project on turtles once. Ever notice how slowly they move, and yet they can swim up to twelve miles an hour.

I wouldn't know, she said. I've never seen one swim.

Not even on TV?

Well ya, she said. And once at a pet store.

I mean the big ones. The really old ones. The ones you can sit on, I said.

I was lying in the surf looking up at all the bruises on her legs. She was so beautiful and so bashed up. It made me sad. I stuck my face into the salty water. If only I could take in a deep breath, sprout gills and live at the bottom of the ocean.

I gotta go, she said suddenly. My dad'll start wondering where I am. He doesn't like me to be on my own for too long.

You're not on your own, I said. You're with me.

But he doesn't know that, does he.

Will I see you later?

Ya, she said. I dunno. Maybe, and she turned to go.

I watched as she made less headway than the effort it took to march across the sand and back towards the road. I watched her ass in her shorts and the tops of her thighs as the waves pushed me up onto the beach then pulled me back in again, caressing me forward and back. I sighed and turned onto my back and felt the sun on my belly like a pancake. Salt water rushed up the legs of my shorts, trapping the air inside and making them billow out like parachutes. I felt the sand shift and mould itself around my body.

Anna, I said out loud to myself. Anna. Anna. Anna.

That evening I met Derrick on Alta Way, walking out of town towards the highway. Derrick was two years older than me, although we were in the same class at junior high, and always wore the sweatshirts that his father brought back from conventions across the States. His father was a consultant for some sporting goods manufacturer and made a pretty good living. I only ever saw him once, driving through town in a Buick with all the windows down. I'd never seen Derrick react so quickly, but when his father leaned out of the window and hollered at him to get on home, Derrick took off like an Olympic sprinter. When his dad was away, which was most of the time, Derrick was just like the rest of us kids in town. Latchkey kids. We spent most of our time outdoors, and nobody's mother ever came looking or called us in for dinner. We were like hoboes, rootless and unreliable. If the wind had carried us away, we'd have been happy. At some point, I think we'd all had the same dream of leaving Round Bay and going somewhere else. I guess in that way I felt connected to them, more out of circumstance than by choice. But on the whole, they were tougher and more worldly than me, although I did manage to win their respect for being able to dive off Adam's Point, a feat even Derrick was too chicken to attempt.

Derrick pulled a mickey of whiskey out of his pocket and handed it to me. I took a swig. He asked me if I wanted to go down to the highway and play a game. I agreed and followed him. It was growing dark and in the distance I could see headlights streaking through the trees. Derrick was wired, wired for anything that had a little evil in it, and his idea of a game was to throw rocks at the cars going by. Twenty points a hit.

I was reluctant at first, but after a bit more whiskey, I started to warm to the idea. I felt safe and invisible crouched in the bushes, beyond the reach of the cars' high beams. The sky was clear and there wasn't even a hint of a breeze. I picked up a pebble and launched it at a family wagon. I heard a ping and saw the driver turn his head. A small head popped up in the back seat as the car swerved slightly in its lane. I giggled. It was funny. I never thought of the danger.

Derrick hurtled a larger rock, the size of a golf ball, then doubled over with laughter. See that heap of junk? he said. I'm sure I cracked the windshield with that one. What a shot . . .

That heap of junk, I said, is slowing down. Derrick stood up and we watched as the car pulled over. Four doors immediately opened and four Mexicans jumped out, shouting in Spanish and running towards us.

Fuck! I screamed.

Run! Derrick yelled and we bolted like rabbits through the trees.

I looked back and they were on our tail. We had the advantage of knowing the terrain, but two of the Mexicans were fast runners. I could hear them yelling at us but didn't understand the language. We ran full-out for five minutes. We cut across a mowed field and onto a dirt road that wound down to the ocean. My heart was pounding but the ground kept flying underneath me. When we got to the path that led up to the point, we split up. Derrick disappeared to the left, down towards the beach, and I headed straight for the cliffs. I knew the Mexicans could see me up ahead, scrambling over the rocks, and heard their voices as they slowed down and regrouped. They were panting heavily and whispering among themselves. I could tell they thought they had me cornered.

When I got to the top, I ran to the edge and looked down. The water was calm and I could hear the ocean as it nudged the coastline. I tried to slow my breathing, taking in great gulps of air and holding it in. I swung around when I heard the first man clamber over the rim. I could see his teeth gleaming in the moonlight and the sweat on his forehead shone like Vaseline. When all four men had gathered at the top, they started to surround me, inching their way forward with their knees slightly bent and their arms outstretched like they were trying to catch a stray dog. I heard a wave roll in and waited for the silence before it fizzled and folded in on itself. It met the immovable resistance of the shore, ruptured and shrank back into the sea. I gave them the finger, spun around and threw myself off the edge, screaming the only two words I knew in Spanish.

Gringo! Cerveza!

[32]

I didn't even have time to take my runners off. I buckled up in midair and grabbed hold of them, hitting the water like a cannonball, knowing full well my dad'd be furious if I lost another pair of shoes.

It seemed like ages before I pulled my body, dripping and heavy with wet clothes, back onto dry land. I heard a whistle and saw the flames of a campfire at the other end of the beach. I waved and slowly made my way towards it, feeling the heat of the still-warm sand under my feet. Occasionally, I looked up at the stars and felt the distance between myself and them. When Derrick came to meet me with his mickey of whiskey, I realized how cold I was and took a couple of hits to warm up.

Derrick slapped me on the back and said, That was the coolest, man. I watched the whole thing from down here. They couldn't fucken believe it. Kept staring down at the water, but of course they couldn't see you from up there. And then after a few minutes they started arguing and waving their arms around, and then they just took off. Like they thought you were dead or somethin'. It was fucken amazing. Give this guy a beer, he said as we approached the fire. Ben, get John a beer!

I sat down by the fire and nodded to Ben and he started rummaging through a knapsack on his lap. Babe smiled at me and I could tell she was drunk as usual. Maureen came over and put a towel around my shoulders.

You'd better get out of those wet things, she said, squeezing my arms.

I'm okay, I said.

[33]

Suit yourself. But don't blame me if you catch pneumonia.

What are you? Derrick asked. His fucken mother?

Fuck you, she said.

I'm okay, really, I said, rubbing my hair with the towel. So how 'bout that beer?

Sure, Ben said. Here, catch.

I guzzled one, then another beer, and sat listening to them argue, staring into the flames and thinking about Anna. I propped my sneakers up against a charred log and watched the steam rise out of them as they started to heat up. Babe leaned back and fell over and couldn't stop laughing. Ben straddled her and put his hand over her mouth. Derrick turned on a portable radio and Maureen got up and stepped out of the ring of light, beyond the orange glow of the fire, and started to dance. Her skin looked blue, even her white t-shirt looked blue. The sand blue-grey. The sky blue-black.

I shivered and moved closer to the fire. My clothes were still wet and clung to my skin. If I sat still and didn't move they felt warm enough, but I wanted to get up. I wanted to be on my own so that I could concentrate on Anna. I kept going over our first meeting in my mind. It was almost a burden or a chore the way I had to relive the conversation over and over again, making sure I remembered everything exactly the way it happened, cursing myself for all the stupid things I'd said, thinking of all the things I wished I had said. I stood up feeling drunk and dizzy and decided to walk it off.

Hey! Where you going? Derrick asked.

I'll be back, I said and shoved my feet into my hot, wet running shoes.

I walked away from the fire and felt the air turn cool. I

weaved my way towards the other end of the beach where the rocks rose up sheer as a wall. I put my forehead against the smooth, cold stone and rested my whole weight. My eyes were closed when I felt a hand on my shoulder.

John?

I turned around. Oh hi, Maureen. Whaddya want?

Wanna kiss?

Aw, come off it, Maureen. Not now. I feel sick.

Come on, John, she said, leaning into me.

I'm not in the mood, I said.

Just shut up, she said. Don't talk.

She put her mouth against mine and opened her lips and forced her tongue against my teeth.

Open your mouth, she said and I did. She tasted like cigarettes and alcohol. She started moaning and rubbing her body against mine. She took my hand and brought it up to her breast.

Come on, John, she said and her hand went down and unzipped my shorts. She reached inside my underwear.

Don't, I said, but she persisted. She touched my penis and it reacted, all on its own without me wanting it to. I could feel myself getting hard so I pushed her away and she snickered.

What's the matter, John? Can't get it up?

Knock it off, Maureen.

Don't you like me?

Give it up.

What's the matter, baby?

I'm not your fucken baby, I said, and she started to laugh.

You always were a little queer.

Shut up, I said, and Maureen came forward and tried to

[35]

kiss me again. Get off of me! I yelled and grabbed her by the arms and squeezed them hard.

Ouch, she said.

What's the matter, Maureen? I thought you wanted it, I said and pushed her up against the rocks.

Get off me, you pig.

Oh, so now I'm a pig, I said and raised my knee up to her crotch. She let out a whimper. I turned my face and shut my eyes and kneed her again, harder this time.

Stop it, John. It's not funny anymore. Let go of me.

A wave of nausea washed through me and my head felt hot. I let go of her and she stumbled sideways. I doubled over, putting a hand out to the rocks to steady myself.

Just look at you, she said, turning and walking away. You're pathetic.

I slumped to my knees and let my head fall forward onto the sand. I thought about my dad, how mad he got. I never knew why or where it was coming from but after this I knew I had his temper too. I covered my head with my hands. There was nothing good in my life. I was a loser and I hated myself.

The following day, I woke with a headache. I walked slowly into town and sat down on the curb outside Mick's. After a couple of minutes, Anna walked out holding a brown paper bag full of groceries in the oval of her arms. Hi there, she said.

Hi, I said, glancing quickly at her face.

You been down to that cliff today?

What cliff?

Where you dove from yesterday.

What, Adam's Point?

I guess so. If that's what it's called.

Ya, it's named after some rich guy who used to own all the land round here, I said, flicking a stone into the street. The state got it when he died. That's what I heard.

Are you sure it's safe? she asked.

You can't see it from the beach but there's a kind of ledge that you can jump off. That's what makes it so good for diving. The water's really deep. I can't touch the bottom.

You know, John, you're the only person round here who talks to me.

Well, you're the only person round here worth talking to.

You're funny, you know that?

Am I?

Ya, she said and leaned to one side and kicked me in the shins.

I was just about to get up when her father yelled out the window of a rusty green Volvo. Anna! Come on! Let's go!

Anna shrugged and ran over to the car and handed the groceries in through the window. She went round to the other side and got in. I watched as her father spun the tires and sped a little too quickly out of town.

I went down to the beach and worked on the boats, right through the afternoon and into the evening. The barnacles were cracking off easily, falling at my feet. My hands were stinging and burned from the salt where I had sliced the skin on my knuckles and on the tips of my fingers. My stomach was in knots from wrapping around nothing all day so I decided to head home and check the fridge. I waved to Peter who was having a smoke, and left.

The walk home seemed to take longer than usual, and when I got there I headed straight for the kitchen. I opened the fridge door and stared at the empty shelves.

Where you been all day? my father asked and I swung around surprised to see him sitting at the kitchen table.

I didn't see you there, I said.

There's nothing in the fridge.

There never is.

Well, if you helped out a bit more round here instead of expecting me to do all the work, maybe we'd have something to eat.

I'm sorry, I wasn't aware that you did any work at all.

You keep talking like that, son, and I'll . . .

You'll what? I asked.

When the hell did you become so lippy, eh? You used to be such a nice kid. So quiet, he said into his glass of bourbon. I've done my best for you, you know. It hasn't been easy on my own.

You haven't been *on your own*.

He raised one eyebrow.

Well, you haven't, have you?

What the fuck are you talking about? he asked.

You know what I'm talking about.

Those women don't count, he said, his voice quivering with restraint. Besides, that's none of your goddamn business.

You're the one who makes it my business. You're the one who brings them home. It's not my fault if I hear what goes on. I can't help it if I hear their stupid fucken voices. Ooh, Orin, I teased, rubbing my hands all over my chest and moving my hips from side to side. Ooh baby, don't stop. Do it again. It feels so good . . .

Shut up! he yelled and stood up, knocking his chair backwards onto the floor.

How d'you think that makes me feel, eh?

I said shut up!

No wonder mom left, I murmured under my breath.

What did you say?

Nothing, I said, backing towards the door.

Nothing is right! You don't know shit, he said, placing his hands on the table and leaning forward, his hair, unwashed and greying at the temples, falling down across his face. You have no idea what happened. You can't even remember her. You were too damn young.

I do so remember her!

What the hell's gotten into you lately.

I'm not a child anymore. I know what you get up to. You're a bum. A fucken lazy bum and you embarrass me!

How dare you speak to me like that!

I'm ashamed of you, dad. There. I said it. I wish you would just leave me alone.

I'll leave you alone, alright. I'll leave you so fucken alone you won't even remember what it's like to have a father!

Fine! I shouted. I can't even remember what it's like to have one already!

Get the fuck out of my sight, John, before I thump you!

Go on, I sneered.

Get out! he yelled and lunged at me and I turned and ran into my bedroom and slammed the door.

I sat down on my bed. I held my hands out in front of me

and they were shaking. I heard my dad stomping around the house, swearing to himself and knocking things over. I heard the screen door crack shut and then there was silence. I could hear myself breathe. My cheeks felt hot and I could feel the sweat under my arms. I walked over to the door and opened it slowly. I peered out, ventured down the hallway and back into the kitchen.

I went over to the window and looked outside. My dad was walking down the driveway with my bicycle slung over his shoulder by the crossbar.

Bastard, I swore and ran out of the house after him. He turned around when he heard me coming. I ran straight for his waist like a football linebacker. He had just enough time to make a fist and hold it out to meet my face. It hit me right in the eyeball and like a cartoon character my head snapped back and then my body and finally my legs and feet. I landed on my back and saw a white bird suspended in the blue jello of the sky.

But it's mine, I said to no one in particular.

Not anymore it ain't, he said and then he walked off, taking my 5-speed racing bike with him.

The next time I saw Anna I was shuffling through town kicking pebbles on the pavement with my fists thrust deep into the back pockets of my jeans. I pulled my baseball cap down over my eyes.

Hey, John, how ya been?

Fine.

Where ya been?

Around.

Whatchya been doing?

Does it matter?

Not really.

Good. 'Cause that seems to be the general consensus.

Feeling sorry for yourself?

So what if I am? I got reason to, I said and raised my face to look at her.

That's quite a shiner you got there. How'd you get it?

How'd you bust up your lip? I asked, noticing that her mouth was bruised and swollen.

Ya, well, we've all got problems. C'mon, John. Let's go get a piece of pie. Still haven't tried the cherry.

Anna dropped the corners of her mouth and gave me a look that said, Oh my God, not the cherry! and it made me laugh. Then she reached out her hand and, leaning on my shoulder, kissed me softly on the cheek.

I'd do anything for her, I thought to myself. Slay dragons for her.

We were coming out of Shirley's, squinting in the sun and patting our bellies full of cherry pie, when someone knocked my baseball cap off from behind and shoved me sideways. Derrick, Ben, Maureen and Babe surrounded us like gangsters chewing gum, looking everywhere but directly at Anna, like she wasn't even there.

Hey, Johnny. Long time no see. Whatchya been doing?

Hi, Derrick.

What happened to your face?

Never mind about that, I said.

Hey John, Maureen said, winking and behaving just the

same as ever, as if nothing had ever happened between us. I'm having a party tonight. Wanna come?

I dunno, Maureen. I looked at Anna who was staring at the ground. She turned her head and looked up the street. I don't think so, I said.

Aw, come on. My parents aren't gonna be there. We got a two-four and Ben's older brother said he'd get us two more. First real party of the summer and everybody's gonna be there.

She came real close to me as she was talking, put her arm around my waist so that I could feel her breast on the back of my shoulder. Come on, Johnny. It'll be the party of the year.

You're such a slut, Maureen.

Shut up, Derrick. You're just jealous.

Fuck you!

Fuck you!

Would you two just shut up! Ben shouted and he put himself between Maureen and Derrick who were sparring like two cocks in a pen.

I sighed.

Are you gonna come? Ben asked. You can bring your girlfriend.

What girlfriend? Maureen spat the words out. Her?

Everybody turned and looked at Anna. The muscles at the back of her jaw tightened and flexed like biceps.

Got a problem? Anna asked, looking at Derrick whose mouth was hanging open.

Told ya, Ben said.

You'll have to bring your own booze, Maureen said. It's not like we have enough beer for just anybody who wants to come.

[42]

I've got a bottle of Jack Daniels, Anna said.

No, you don't.

Yes, I do.

You're lying.

Why would I be lying?

Where'd you get it?

My dad.

Your dad's gonna give you a bottle of Jack Daniels?

So?

Jesus Christ. What kind of family do you come from?

Better than yours, I expect.

What's that supposed to mean?

Oh, nothing. Just a hunch.

Who is this girl? Maureen asked.

Look, we'll see you at the party, okay John? Ben said and started walking off, pulling Maureen after him. Bring the girl, he said over his shoulder.

Maureen clucked her tongue and said to me, I'll see *you* there later.

Babe followed on her heels. Derrick slapped me hard on the back and said, She wants you, man. Boy does she ever, then ran after Babe. When he reached her, he grabbed her by the waist and started humping her from behind while she shrieked, Stop! Stop it! and they all dissolved into laughter and the dust rose like a dervish round their sneakers and carried them away. Anna and I were left standing there, holding our tummies, but this time it was because we felt shy and awkward and separate from each other and didn't know how we could ever laugh for no reason again or touch each other innocently.

[43]

You should go, you know, Anna said. To the party.

But I don't want to.

But you have to.

Why?

Because they're your friends.

Some friends, I said.

Still . . .

I won't go without you.

Scared?

I'm not like them.

Really?

Will you come with me?

Maybe, she said. I'd have to get drunk first, though.

We arranged to meet at the bottom of her street. I arrived early and was sitting on the curb bent over writing her name in the dirt, when two black sandals appeared in front of my hands. I looked up. Anna's hair was pinned back to one side with a blue barrette in a way I'd never seen before and it made her look older. She was wearing a dark blue t-shirt and a short black skirt. There was a silver chain around her neck.

I held her ankles and looked at her toes. I counted each one of them before getting up.

You sure you wanna go? I asked. They're gonna give you a hard time.

I'll take it as my initiation, she said. I'm used to it. Every time we move to a new place it's like this. It's like moving to a new school halfway through the year. I've done that three times. You have to get up in class and introduce yourself. Then the teacher asks you what your parents do and that's when I have to explain that I only live with my father, and for the rest of the class everybody's whispering about me, and when the bell rings, I get interrogated in the school yard. You get used to it. You figure out what to say. To please them. And you find out who everybody's scared of and you go to that person first and whether it means you have to steal something from the store or cheat on a test or smoke a joint or get drunk, you do it. Just to impress the toughest person there. And generally after that things are okay.

You're too good and smart for them, you know.

I know, she said. But this is my new life. So let's just go and get it over with. Show them we're not intimidated.

We walked all the way to Maureen's in silence. Anna kept taking swigs from the bottle of Jack Daniels she'd brought in a paper bag and passing it to me. When we got there, the place was throbbing. Every window in the house was lit and shadows passed behind the glass. A beer bottle rolled off the porch and a boy ran out the door, leaned up against a tree in the front yard and puked. Something was playing on the stereo. It stopped abruptly. Someone shouted and the music started up again. Anna squeezed my hand and I had to look away because mine was cold and clammy.

We approached the party like lion tamers. If we'd had whips we would have used them. The walls were pulsating, almost sweaty inside, and the air was a soup of smoke. We waded into the livingroom. There were lots of people there I'd never seen before. I saw Ben's older brother smoking something in a dark corner with his arm around a woman. He had his hand inside her blouse. I asked Anna for another shot and she handed me the bottle and I stripped it of its tattered bag. I took a large swallow. My mouth then my neck and shoulders contracted as the liquid punched me in the back of the throat. I thought of my dad lying on his bed with that photograph pinned to his chest. The smell of bourbon. I think I wanted my mother then, some vague notion of mother, like when you're sick and tired and all your muscles go slack and you want someone to scrape your toast or bring you a glass of ginger ale. But maybe it wasn't so great after all. To have some fat, slobbering mother like Maureen's. Someone else to fuck you up.

Anna took out a cigarette and ripped a match from her pack. I noticed her hands were shaking and her eyes looked glassy.

Let's mingle, she said and pulled me down the hall towards a dark doorway. We walked into another room, the TV room, where a few guys were sitting around the stereo, putting on records and arguing about the music. Every time they came across an album they didn't like, they snapped it in two. The floor was littered with the black half-circles of broken records.

I looked at Anna and her eyelids were fluttering. Jerks, she said. Let's go find your friends.

We walked into the kitchen where Derrick was bent over the stove doing hot knives. Someone from our highschool was holding the knives. He was a grade ahead of us and I didn't know his name. There was a row of little pieces of hash lined up on the counter and he'd touch the red tip of a knife to one and it would stick and he'd press the other knife on top and it would disappear in a puff of smoke. Derrick was holding an empty toilet paper roll to his mouth like an enormous cardboard cigar, funnelling the smoke and sucking it in.

Hey kids, he said, looking up and grinning through a red circle around his lips, making an effort to raise his eyelids. You been gone so long, thought you'd never come.

We just got here, I said.

Wanna puff?

No thanks.

How 'bout you? he asked Anna.

Why not? she said and took the cardboard tube from him. The guy with the knives branded another piece of hash and held it up to her. She drank in all the smoke like a real pro. I felt proud of her and then immediately felt I didn't have the right. I wanted to touch her. The kitchen lights swirled in her hair as she tossed her head back.

So what's your name? the guy with the knives asked her.

Anna.

What's yours? I asked, trying to get his attention.

Jake, he replied, without taking his eyes off her. Where you from?

Boston, she said.

And your parents?

My dad's Greek.

And your mom?

She's American.

Is she as beautiful as you?

More.

I can't believe that.

Try.

Alright boys and girls, Derrick interrupted, because he couldn't stand not being the centre of attention. How 'bout another hit, Jake? Or are you too busy right now?

Look here, penis breath, it's my dope and I'll share it with who and when I choose. Got it?

Sure buddy. Just inquiring.

Wannanother toke, Anna?

I think I'm gonna go find the bathroom.

Finally she turned to me and asked, Do you know where it is?

I think it's upstairs. I gotta go too.

You don't have to come with me. I'll be fine on my own.

I felt self-conscious after that and stood there with my arms crossed, staring at the wall and trying to seem preoccupied.

You're hooked, man, Derrick said after Anna had left the kitchen. Like a fish, man. What does her old man do?

He's a writer.

What kind of a writer?

I dunno.

What's that funny last name of hers?

It's not funny. It's Greek, I said.

How long's she staying?

How the fuck am I supposed to know?

Sen-si-tive.

I turned to leave just as Maureen was coming in. She was wearing a pink tank top that showed off her tits and a pair of tight white pants. She wasn't wearing any shoes. She could barely stand up and leaned on me when she got near enough to whisper in my ear, Why don't you like me, John?

I do like you.

No, you don't. Not the way you like her.

Who? I asked ridiculously.

You know. The new girl.

Maybe I like her. Maybe I don't.

Then why don't you give me a kiss. Right now.

Aw, come off it, Maureen. Stop buggin' me.

See? You hate me.

I don't hate you.

Then why don't you want to kiss me?

This is stupid, Maureen.

Oh, so now I'm stupid, is that it?

I mean this isn't going anywhere.

Well, it's not my fault.

Look, I'm not interested, and I like you less when you're like this, Maureen.

Ah, but I like her better this way, Derrick said and pulled her over and held her tight.

You guys make me sick, I said and left the kitchen and started making my way upstairs. I saw Ben passed out on the floor near the stairs. His mouth was hanging open and he was drooling. Some girl was curled up next to him. Her t-shirt stuck out in front because her arms were crossed and she was lying on her side. I could see the top of her white bra and I thought of Anna. I was thinking about her knees and elbows and her mouth when I nearly got knocked over by this older guy careening down the stairs, zipping up his fly and muttering under his breath. I got to the landing and the bathroom was locked. A door to the left was slightly ajar and I saw Anna sitting on a bed. Her face was lit from the hall light and I could see the outline of her cheek. I stood outside the door and watched. She was stroking something on the bed and then I realized it was Babe.

Babe was lying on her side like a sow, clutching her knees to her chest and whimpering.

Are you okay? I heard Anna say. Do you want me to get someone?

Babe only whimpered some more and brought her knees up closer to her body.

Why don't you just sleep it off. You'll feel better in the morning.

Anna laid her fingertips gently on Babe's temples. Babe closed her eyes and stuck her thumb in her mouth. Anna looked around, then picked up a blanket that was lying on the floor. She shook it out over the bed and pulled it up to Babe's chin and paused, then pulled it right over her head the way you cover up a dead body.

She came out of the room and said, John, I don't know her but I feel sorry for her. Let's get outta here.

We walked out of the house and left the chaos of the party behind.

What a mess, Anna said. It worries me.

They're idiots, I said. Who cares what happens to them.

That's just it, John. Nobody does. You can't blame them.

Well, I do.

Well, you shouldn't.

Why not?

Because you're judging them. My dad says nobody has the right to judge anybody else.

What if they're acting like total fucken assholes?

They probably have their reasons.

I dunno. I think you're being too generous.

Just wait till you're on the other end.

I won't be.

Ha! Anna laughed. Don't be so confident.

I wish I was, I said.

Why?

Because I'd kiss you.

Go on, she said and came over and stood close to me. I put my lips to hers and alarms started going off inside my body. I felt the world tilt and spin, my skin grow prickles.

Walk me home, she said and I was so light-headed that I had to keep touching tree trunks the whole way back just to keep from losing my balance.

The night was finally peaceful. The air creaking with crickets. The buzz of cicadas like high voltage wires overhead. We arrived at her house and the lights were still on.

I looked at Anna and her eyelids were doing that strange fluttering business I'd seen at the party. I kissed her again. That's all I did. I kissed her. It was easy and she let me. Then she took a step backward and swayed a bit, staring past me like she was day-dreaming. The air was cool and I could smell the evergreens in her front yard.

I've got an idea, she said after a while. But you'll have to trust me.

I held my hand over my heart and tried to look solemn.

Anna held a finger to her lips and motioned for me to follow her. We crouched and ran like snipers over to the car in her driveway. Get in, she whispered. The door's unlocked.

Are we going somewhere?

Yep.

Have you got a key?

Ya, I keep a copy. Sometimes my dad lets me drive. Last week we went to Capitola and my dad asked me to drive home 'cause he'd been drinking. On the back streets, of course.

I don't think I like your father.

You don't know him.

Still. Have you got a license?

They won't give me one.

Anna released the park brake and the car began to roll. We rolled out into the street, then Anna turned the key in the ignition and started the car.

Where are we going?

Relax, she said.

We took the main route out of town, past Shirley's, and turned onto a dirt road that ran parallel to the highway, through the woods then out into open farmland. The earth was hard-packed and the car seemed to float around corners and over the rises. I could feel the booze sloshing around in my stomach. The smell of strawberries wafted into the car through the vents on the dashboard. Anna wound her window down and the wind caught her hair. Her face looked eerie in the blue light from the instrument panel.

Open your window too, Anna whispered. And the back ones.

I straddled the front seat and flopped into the back. I rolled down the windows and sat for a while with my sweaty palms resting flat on the cool leather and stared at the back of her head. Her hair flickered like bats in a cave. Her neck was tanned. I reached forward and touched it.

Get back up here, she said. And I did. Watch this, she said. And I did.

She turned off the headlights and we coasted through the dark. I couldn't take my eyes off the road but wanted to feel her sitting next to me. I put out my hand and felt her thigh. The muscle tightened as she accelerated up an incline. We crested the hill and she turned the engine off and we plunged down the road, turned left, then right, and drifted to a halt on a long, flat stretch. We sat there in the buzzing dark. The crickets and the rustling wheat alive all around us. We sat there and felt the dome of the sky above and the hard-packed earth below.

I turned to Anna and said, I love you.

She shivered. Her whole body a sudden spasm that broke the stillness.

Are you okay? I asked but she didn't answer me. She only started the car and did a skillful U-turn in the road and sped back to town. I was confused but didn't have much time to think about what was confusing me because she drove like a maniac through the streets and I was sure we were gonna get caught or have an accident. I didn't say anything although I wanted to tell her to slow down. I just sat there and kept my mouth shut. She leaned forward and peered through the windshield as if she were driving through thick fog. Her hands left sweaty marks on the steering wheel that glistened in the dark. I wanted to take control, wrench the hand brake or pull her foot off the accelerator. I wanted her to stop but I couldn't move. We sped past Shirley's at an illegal speed and through the empty streets to her house. We took the last corner on an angle. I'm sure the left wheels actually lifted off the ground and the tires made a terrible screeching sound. A dog started barking and then another one. Anna didn't slow down as we approached her place. She missed the driveway and drove up onto the lawn. We hit a tree and crashed.

Anna started fiddling with the door handle. She started thrashing around when she couldn't get it open. Her dad came running from the house screaming, What the fuck is going on! Where have you been? He ripped the car door open and she fell out onto her side.

Baba! Baba!

He picked her up and flung her over his shoulder like a fireman and walked back into the house.

The door slammed. The porch light went out. All the lights on the first floor went out. I saw the shadow of her father mount the stairs. Anna was flailing in his arms. The light in her bedroom went on and the two shadows fell to the floor. After that, nothing moved. Everything was silent. There was nothing more to see and the house gave nothing away. Just one bright square of light shining from her bedroom window. After a while this light went out too.

I was still sitting in the car leaning over to the driver's side watching the house through the frame of the open car door. I sat up and leaned against the seat. My back was damp and cold and I was trembling. The hood was buckled up so bad that I couldn't see over it. The engine still hissed and steamed. My head hurt. I opened the door and forced myself to stand and suddenly felt nauseous. I puked near the front tire. Then I stood for a very long time with my arms hanging at my sides staring back at the house, like it was a skull with dark recesses where the eyes used to be. I lifted a hand to my forehead and felt a lump like half an orange beneath the skin.

My eyes welled up with tears and the house disappeared into a blur like it was sinking. I forced my mouth down and stretched my face to drain the tears from my eyes so that it would come back into focus. I didn't want to lose sight of it. I needed that house then. I was afraid that if I looked away it might just disappear and take Anna away with it.

I stood there shivering until I noticed that the sky was growing light and different noises taking over. I felt the dew rise up to meet the sun. It was the coldest time of day and my body felt rigid. I heard the familiar sound of a screen door thwacking back into place and a car start. Somewhere, a baby began to cry.

I found myself on the top of Adam's Point staring out at the water and listening to the mocking caw of those good-for-nothing seagulls. I knew the salt water would cool my head. I didn't jump off the edge, I simply fell. Stiff as a board, fell. And when I hit the water my heart cracked open and my lungs seized up. I couldn't breathe. I needed breath. I broke my own rule and I panicked.

The cold knocked it out of me. My leg cramped up and I lost all sense of direction. It was dark and the waves tossed me around like I was in some giant washing machine. I pulled the water in heart-shaped patterns, desperately kicking my one good leg until finally, just as my lungs were about to burst, the sea turned bottle-green above me and I headed up for air.

I swam out to where the waves undulated gently beneath the surface, the ocean stretched to the horizon like a black plastic tarp. I was exhausted. I felt at odds with the sea, like I was being punished for something I didn't know. For a long time I lay on my back like an otter, with my hands folded on my stomach until I felt strong enough to swim again. I floated there until I was so cold that I could no longer feel my skin and all the turquoise in the sky had turned to peach.

I didn't see Anna for days after that. The car eventually got towed and new grass laid down like rolls of carpet. Every day seemed longer than the last and every day my hatred for her father grew. I wasn't even sure if anybody was home. The curtains were always drawn. The porch light off in the evenings and only a faint green light shone from the living-room windows.

I stayed out of the water all that week and worked on Peter's boat, sanding down the hull to a smooth, raw finish. All I had left to do was give it a paint job and I could start in on my own. Lil was in bad shape. The bench wouldn't have supported even my weight but the hull was pretty solid. The gunnel was chipped and needed some wood filler. One of the rowlocks was missing, but I could get one easily enough from Peter in exchange for some odd jobs. Lil lay on her side behind the boathouse while the sun peeled the last strands of paint off her body. I tended to the other boat like I had all the time in the world. I had the rest of my life, and it was during that week that I almost gave up on Anna and let the boredom and hopelessness of my nowhere-going town infect me. It was like I knew I couldn't be a hero then. Couldn't save her from her father or even help myself.

I kicked garbage cans that week, ripped leaves off trees and threw stones. I even snapped at Shirley and said, You're not my fucken mother, which upset her pretty bad seeing as she didn't deserve it. Finally, I couldn't bear it any longer and approached Anna's house with the intention of knocking on

[56]

her door. It was late and the air was so balmy you couldn't feel it on your skin as you moved through it. The house was dark and still among the still branches of the trees all around it. The garden was well kept except for the scar where the new grass had been laid out in strips to cover the tire tracks. They had turned a brownish yellow and looked like Band-Aids on the lawn. It made me think of Anna's bruises and I grew angry and wanted to confront her father, but I knew nothing about him or his strength or his temper. My anger gave me courage but it was mixed with fear. A fear of all fathers.

That eerie green light still glowed in the window. A white lace curtain billowed softly in a crossdraft coming from the livingroom. I climbed the three steps up to the porch, walked quietly over to the window and peered inside. Her father was bent over a desk with his head in his hands. A small lamp with a dark green shade was perched on the table. It was the kind of lampshade I'd seen in the movies, hanging above card tables where gangsters played poker and smoked Havana cigars. His hair was dark like Anna's, only a bit curlier, and still as thick as a young man's. He dropped his hand and picked up a pen. He wrote something down on a piece of paper. He stopped abruptly, crossed out what he had written and started again. He took a fresh piece of paper, copied something from the first then dropped that page onto the floor. The floor was strewn with paper. In fact, the whole room was stuffed with books and folders and stacks of magazines. He stared at the page on his desk. He seemed frustrated and yet, when he raised his face and suddenly caught my eye, there was a tenderness in the way his mouth relaxed almost immediately.

[57]

Hi there, he said, smiling gently.

Ya, hi, I replied.

Can I help you? he asked.

I want to see Anna.

And you are?

John, I said.

John! Come in. Come round the front door. I was wondering when I'd meet you. I thought it might be sooner. Please come in, he said, rising from his chair and waiting for me to move. When I didn't, he asked, Do you want a drink or something?

Is she alright?

Anna? Yes, yes. She's fine. We were talking about you today. I thought it might be nice to have you round for dinner. She wanted to talk to you, but then she realized she doesn't even have your phone number.

That's right, I said.

She hasn't been well enough to leave the house, you understand. How does tomorrow sound? Can you make it? Would you like to come in and have a drink?

No, that's okay. I just wanted to make sure she was alright. I just needed to know. Can I see her?

She's asleep.

Oh.

So, will you come for dinner?

Ya, I guess so, I said.

How does eight o'clock sound?

Fine.

Great . . . Well, we'll see you tomorrow then.

I nodded. Okay.

Right, he said. See you then.

Goodbye, I said.

Goodbye, John.

I almost bowed as I backed away from the window. I was confused. He had spoken so kindly, like he really was, but you never can tell.

Eight o'clock sharp and I arrived like the nutcracker ready to crack this thing open, overly formal and awkward in a change of clothes. I was wearing my only pair of dress pants and a button-down shirt. I had combed my hair and even shaved my chin and upper lip with my dad's razor. My nails shone like shells slightly luminous and blue underwater. The door was open and I knocked on the frame before stepping inside and calling hello.

In here, John, her father answered. I ventured into the livingroom where he was propped up at his desk with half-moon glasses on his nose and a big hardback book lying open under the green lamp. He didn't look up when I came in but let out a deep sigh.

What are you reading? I asked.

An etymological dictionary.

A what?

It gives the roots of words.

Whaddya mean?

Where a word comes from. Its origin. Words are constantly changing. They have a history, right? And I like to know what a word meant originally. It can give it a whole new connotation.

I guess so.

Take this for instance. Do you know the root of the word diabolical, John?

Are you being serious?

It's Greek. Dia, meaning through. Bollo, to throw. To throw through. To divide. The force or motion of that which splits something apart. Gives the word an interesting twist, don't you think? Forget some superstitious notion about the devil, which is how it's commonly defined, from a Christian point of view, because the roots of the word existed before Christ. The Greeks defined it in terms of a schism, the splitting up of something whole, like two lovers being wrenched apart. Now that's an awful thing to think about, he said, looking up at me and waiting, like he wanted me to help him out. I couldn't care less about the devil, he continued. But to be separated from something that is a part of you, that you need or love, now that's tragic. That's diabolical.

Hm, I said, when he had finished.

Ah, but enough of this, he said and clapped the book shut. He got up and walked towards me, held out his hand and said, How are you, John? I'm sorry about last week. I don't even remember seeing you in the car. I was out of my mind about Anna. That was some parking job she did. Did you get hurt?

Not really.

I'm not very good in emergency situations. I tend to freeze up. Can't think straight. I prefer the safety of books. Anna tells me you like to read.

Comics, mainly.

Everything I've ever learned, I've learned from books.

Everything?

Well, a helluva lot. I hate the thought that people read less and less. Books are so important, John.

I'll try to remember that, sir.

Please, call me Nick. We don't tend to stand on ceremony around here. Are you hungry?

I'm starving.

Do you like fish?

Yah.

Good, because we're having tuna. Bought some fresh in town from a guy called Foxy.

I know the one.

I'm just going to check on the potatoes. I'll get Anna and the two of you can set the table. Okay?

Yep.

Want something to drink? How 'bout a little beer, just to liven things up, he said and winked.

I smiled briefly and he left the room. I sat down on the sofa then got up again. I walked over to the bookshelf and stared at the row of spines without reading a single title. I walked over to the desk and switched the lamp off, then on again.

Hi, John, I heard Anna say and swung around to face her. How've you been?

Alright, I said. What about you?

Fine.

Were you sick?

Ya, I was sick.

Whatcha have?

Just a flu. Nothing serious. I feel better now.

Did he hit you?

Who?

Your dad.

No!

But I saw . . .

You saw nothing, John. And if you wanna stay for dinner I suggest you just drop it right now. I'm fine.

Neither of us spoke until the silence started ringing in my ears. I said, What happened? Did I upset you?

No, she said.

I shouldn't have said anything. I should've kept my big mouth shut.

It wasn't you, she said.

Ya, but you got all weirded out after I said . . .

Let's just forget about it, okay?

But I don't want to forget about it, I said.

Please, John, Anna pleaded, so earnestly that I really wanted to change the subject but something compelled me to continue.

Did you get into trouble about the car?

Well, he confiscated my key.

And?

And what? That's it, John. Stop prying.

I just wish I could do something . . .

How 'bout setting the table? I heard her father say.

I looked over and saw Nick standing in the doorway with a beer in one hand and a dishtowel slung over his shoulder. In his other hand, he was holding a wooden spoon.

Here's your beer, young man.

Thanks, I said and looked back at Anna but she was already heading into the diningroom. Her father watched her walk past, following her with his eyes. I went in after her, feeling the cold wet bottle slipping through my fingers.

*

Dinner was served on ceramic plates with yellow and blue flowers painted in broad strokes around the edge. Big, thick plates and big portions of fish and potatoes and salad. The food was delicious. I'd never tasted anything like it. Anna's father seemed happy and placed his hand on her shoulder when he put down her plate and often patted her arm as he was talking. She seemed distracted, almost sullen, and it seemed to take an effort for her to be cheerful. It was her father and I who did most of the talking. I was still suspicious of his motives and kept looking across at Anna, hoping for a sign. I had to fight the lazy effect the food and the beer and her father's friendly manner was having on me. I felt like I was being drugged.

Nick went out to the kitchen and got three more bottles of beer from the fridge. He came back and sat down. He put his elbows on the table and leaned forward. So you moved here with your father how many years ago?

When I was eight, I said.

And where did you live before that?

Canada. Bella Coola.

Beautiful cool. Sounds nice. Where is it?

Northern BC.

Must've been pretty.

Ya, I guess.

Do you remember it?

Not much.

They're Indians, aren't they?

Who?

The Bella Coola.

That's right. There was an Indian burial ground near my

house. There was this tree they'd hang things from that meant something to the person who was dead. Souvenirs, feathers, jewelry sometimes, and I remember somebody hung a beer can from one of the branches once. There were always lots of cigarette butts on the ground.

A burial ground, huh? Nick repeated.

Ya. It really used to spook me. It was so quiet and empty during the day, but people were always going there at night.

How do you know that? he asked.

Because there'd be ashes from a campfire or more garbage there the next day. I got the same spooky feeling when I went to that abandoned house by the highway. Anna, do you know the one? Past the gas station? There are bits of wallpaper still stuck to the walls. You get a feel for the people who used to live there. Like they had to leave in a hurry and left part of themselves behind.

Maybe I'll check it out one day, he said.

What for? Anna asked.

Why not?

It would be like trespassing.

But nobody lives there anymore.

It's disrespectful, dad.

To whom?

To their memories.

Ah, memory. Now there's a famous topic around here.

But that's exactly what it was like, I said. That's what I felt. I felt like I was trespassing on somebody else's memory. Like the house had its own history, just like a person does. Like the house itself is still alive, except that it feels sick or it's dying, because it's been forgotten. Like it needs people to

[64]

live in it to keep it alive. But not just anybody. The original people. It was like the house wanted its owners back.

Exactly, Anna said.

Yes, well Anna knows all about that, don't you, sweetheart. Pining for the past. Wanting things to go back to the way they were. You see, John, it doesn't just apply to that house of yours, everything has to be remembered in order to be kept alive. If we don't remember things, then they will die. Isn't that your theory, Anna? Memories themselves will die, and then you lose the things that are associated with those memories, most dangerously, people. People you lose. The dearly departed. Those who dare to disappear. Houses might die when they're abandoned, fall into disrepair, but people don't have to. Clinging to the memory of the person who abandoned you isn't gonna do you any favours in the long run, my dear.

So what? Anna said.

But you're carrying around such a heavy burden . . .

Who cares? It's *my* memory . . .

And lest we forget, memory *is* a sacred cow in this house, her father said, raising his beer and toasting the room.

You wouldn't understand, she said. It's personal.

Unreliable, is more like it, he said. The problem is, what we remember is rarely accurate. Especially if it's something we really care about. Then it becomes too subjective.

But if it's all you've got, Anna interrupted, who cares whether it's accurate or not? It's better than nothing.

But that's just the point. It isn't. Can't you see how vulnerable you've made yourself to fantasy and forgetfulness. To delusion! You don't remember the past, you mythologize it.

[65]

I do not, Anna said.

Yes, you do! Your memory is like a shrine, an Indian burial ground. You can't trespass on it. You don't question it. Instead you worship it with morbid obsessiveness. You don't keep it alive, it's what keeps you alive.

That's not true, Anna said. I treasure some memories, but that's only because that's all I've got left. That's all I've got left of my mother, for example, and you know that! Even if they are fucken lousy ones!

Good. Get angry.

Shut up! You just want me to forget so that you can convince me of your version of things. So that you can feel like I've given you my approval to get on with your life. Well, stop waiting for my permission. I'll remember her for as long as I want. I'm not going to give her up just so that you can go screw some fucken student of yours. And you don't have to keep telling me how it's holding me back from getting on with my life because I know!

Anna stopped talking and dropped her head. Her hands were shaking and I could tell her shoulders were as tight as springs. I didn't know what to do. Part of me wanted to protect her and another part of me was afraid to interfere. Nick got up and walked into the kitchen and came out with some more beers. He put one on the table in front of me and one in front of Anna. He raised his hand like he was going to stroke her hair, then let it drop and sat down again. He put his elbows on the table and turned to me.

So what do you remember about your mother, John?

My mother?

Anna told me you don't have a mother, either.

Dad! Maybe he doesn't want to talk about it.

Do you want to talk about it, John?

Not much to talk about really. I don't remember much about her and my dad never talks about it.

Did she run out on you?

I guess you could say that.

Dad! Anna protested again.

No, no, Anna. This is good. Go ahead, John.

What do you want to know?

When did she leave?

When I was eight. That's all. She just left, okay? I dunno. I was young.

Why'd she leave?

She met a guy.

Where?

He came to our house.

The milkman? Nick asked with a grin.

No, I said, without smiling. He was a bum.

A bum?

You know. A beggar.

A beggar. Really . . .?

Look, dad, I think we should talk about something else. I don't want to talk about this.

Why not?

Because!

Anna, one day you're going to have to deal with what your mother did to you. You see, John, Anna's mother also left. For another man. Just packed up and left. It was very hard on Anna. She hasn't learnt to let go. It's a real problem. It depresses me. He turned to Anna and held out his hands, palms up.

When are you going to move on? When are you going to let go?

Like you, dad? The way you just take off? Move to another city when anything bad happens? You don't let go. You run away. You don't deal with things. You avoid them. Ever think what kind of a role model you've been to me? Ever think what all those moves have taught me? Be a coward, Anna. Run away. Don't face up. Don't deal. Just run. You've been teaching me to hightail it out of every difficult situation I've ever been in since mom left.

Anna's dad took another swig of beer. Well, at least I don't mope around feeling sorry for myself, he said. At least I don't internalize things and wait for them to erupt. I don't get so worked up about things to let them ruin my health.

I can't believe you just said that.

Well, for God's sake, Anna. Things can't go on like this forever.

Look, I said. Maybe we should just change the subject.

Oh, now you think so! Anna yelled back at me. It's a bit late, John.

Maybe you could learn something from your friend here, Nick said. He doesn't seem to be so cut up about things.

It was a long time ago, I said. I was very young. I can't even remember what it was like to live with her. You can't expect our experiences to be the same.

It's not the experiences that have to be similar, John. No two people live identical lives. It's how they react that's important. Throw anything my way and I will deal with it. Anna doesn't have the same ability to cope.

Well, can you blame her? Maybe it has something to do

[68]

with you. Maybe you don't give her what she needs to cope. Did you ever think of that?

There was a pause. The room flexed. The air was tense. Nick downed the last of his beer, got up and went over to the cabinet and took out a tumbler and a bottle of brandy. He came back to the table and poured himself a generous shot.

To absent mothers, he said and knocked it back.

I looked over at Anna. She was staring down at her plate, sucking on a strand of hair. She was rocking back and forth, banging the table slightly with her fist. I saw the salt shaker move sideways. A spoon clattered to the floor and I felt pinned by the precision of the noise.

Baba, she said softly. Baba.

Here we go again, her father said. Stay with me, Anna. I'm here.

He turned to me and said, Leave us alone. You can wait in the kitchen.

What? I asked.

Anna stood up. She had a strange grin on her face. She stared right through me with blank, unseeing eyes, almost supernaturally. I didn't know what the fuck was going on.

Go! her dad yelled. Now!

I jumped up and ran over to the kitchen. When I reached the door, I turned around and saw Anna's father go round and hug her. She was on her toes and her arms were rigid. He pressed her firmly against his body and then they slowly spun around like they were doing a waltz. Nick looked up and saw me gaping at them. Shut the goddamn door! he yelled. And so I did.

I laid my forehead against the cool, hard surface of the

door. I heard a struggle. There was a noise like a foot or a hand slapping the hardwood floor. I don't know how long it lasted. My knees felt weak and I slid down onto the floor. I put my ear against the door and heard Anna's rapid breathing and Nick's voice repeating something softly, like he was reassuring her. It's gonna be okay. Just relax. I lay down on my side and pushed my face into the thin space under the door. Through the narrow gap, I could see her leg twitching, pinned down on either side by her father who was lying on top of her. She stopped fighting and the house fell silent.

I waited for what felt like an age. No sound escaped from the diningroom. Eventually, her father stood up and I saw his large shoes next to her bare legs. He walked towards me and tried to open the door but my body was in the way. I moved aside and he came into the kitchen. I caught a glimpse of Anna in the diningroom, lying on the floor with her arms and legs splayed out in four directions. Nick picked me up. I was too weak to resist and he placed me in a chair.

John, he said. Anna has epilepsy.

I stayed for a while longer and then I went home. We didn't talk much but, before I left, Nick told me that he thought I was good for Anna and that he hoped I'd come back. He shook my hand and then he hugged me. Not for very long, but long enough to make my heart race and my breathing shallow. He had strong arms and smelt of tobacco. There was another smell too. Maybe it was Anna's smell that was still on him. It was familiar to me and sweet. It made me horny. When he released me, I had a hard-on which really confused me and I felt ashamed. As I was walking down the steps, he said, See you soon, son.

I wasn't allowed to see Anna for nearly a whole week after that. Despite her father's excuses, I was afraid I'd crossed some kind of line, like she was avoiding me or worse. Eventually, I stopped going round and focussed all my attention on putting the finishing touches on my boat. I asked Peter if I could do some odd jobs in exchange for a rowlock and some pitch to seal the boards in the hull. He said I could do his fish deliveries that day so I rigged the basket, packed with pounds of fresh tuna, to the handlebars of his bike and cycled off. As I made my way towards the hill that would take me up to the big houses where the rich people lived, the ice under the fish slowly melted and trickled down through the spokes and onto the road in drops like blood.

I had never been as far up the hill as I went that day. The road wound up past conifers and rocks and so steeply that I had to get off Peter's bike and push it. I walked for an hour until I could see the sea behind me. I propped the bicycle up against the trunk of a eucalyptus tree and drained the fish box of the ice that had melted. I sat down and watched the water glitter in the bay. I could just make out Adam's Point poking out between the tree tops. I wiped my forehead on the sleeve of my shirt. A garter snake slithered past my shoe and I flicked a pebble at it. The heat was rising up through the soles of my sneakers and the rock underneath me was hot and dry. I could have laid down and slept. I almost did when a shiny, silver Jaguar sped past me kicking up a cloud of dust and disappeared around the bend. I could just make out a blonde head of hair at the wheel and a hand with long red nails dangling down from the window. I got up and continued pushing my bike uphill.

I made a delivery to a Mexican maid in a black and white uniform. *Gracias*, she said and gave me a can of Coke. She took the fish and rinsed it under an outdoor tap then disappeared down a dark passageway around the back of the house. My last delivery was to a Mr Geraldo Marquez at Number One, Hill Drive.

I followed the road until I came to a house at the very top of the hill. It was built in Spanish fashion with red tiles on the roof and low stone walls running up the drive. The door was arched and made of dark, stained wood. It had an ornate iron knocker and a bell rope that you had to pull. The bell rang out a series of notes that echoed on the other side of the door and made the house feel empty. It was a while before anybody answered and I stepped back and peered over at the garage where that silver Jag lay creaking under the blazing sun.

The door opened and a woman answered, wearing a bikini and high heels. I got a blast of cold air. The woman took a drag off her cigarette and exhaled.

Yes? she asked. What do you want?

I've got the fish you ordered, I said.

Deliveries are normally made round the back of the house. I wouldn't be caught dead handling those things, she said, backing away from the damp bundle I was offering. Then the woman looked at me and smiled, or sneered, I couldn't tell which. Her eyes travelled down from my face to my shirt, down my legs to my feet and back up again. Just a minute, she said. Maria! she called into the cavernous house. Your fishmonger's here! The woman looked at me again, shook her head and sighed.

Just then, I heard a voice call gently from within the house, Peter? and a plump, middle-aged woman came rushing towards the door patting her hair into place.

When she saw me, the smile on her face disappeared and her eyes narrowed to two black diamonds in her head. Where's Peter? she asked.

He's down at the boathouse. I'm just doing him a favour.

A favour? she asked. He no want to come? You tell him for me, if he no like to come, I get my fish from someplace else.

And she will, said the woman in the bikini. She no fussy, the woman teased and flicked her cigarette onto the drive. She turned on her high heels and slinked back into the house like a reptile seeking shade under a rock.

Maria's lips quivered and the skin around her mouth went white.

What do you want me to do with this? I asked, holding the fish up again.

Take it back! she snapped. Tell him to bring it hisself, no send little boy to do it for him, and she backed into the house and slammed the door.

I stood on the stoop in the growing odour of fish and stared at the iron knocker in the shape of a lion's head with a ring through its mouth. I turned and walked slowly back to Peter's bicycle. I tucked the lukewarm fish into the basket and coasted the whole way down without pedalling.

When I got to the beach, I took the rejected fish to Peter and placed it on the bench beside him.

What's this? he asked.

Maria didn't want it.

Why not?

She said she'd only take it if you brought it yourself, and that if you didn't, she'd get it from somebody else.

Peter didn't say anything.

She called me a little boy.

Women, he said, shaking his head.

Are you and Maria . . .

Never mind, John. Never you mind, he said and got up and spat and walked into the boathouse and closed the door.

The following morning, I left the house before sunrise and went down to the beach. I watched the sky soften and a pink ridge rise up out of the east. I watched the seagulls glide and swoop down for breakfast. The water looked like tea. I could have taken a cup to it and drunk it. This was the sea I loved. The sand was cool and I dug my heels in. I lay back in a hollow and fell asleep.

In an hour, the sun had risen and was scraping up against me, blistering paint and draining the colour out of comic book covers in storefront windows. I got up on one elbow and looked around. Surveyed the white beach through the flickering grass. The cliffs to my right and Adam's Point sticking out like a crooked finger. The crescent-shaped bay and Peter's boathouse at the other end. I sat up.

A crowd of people started to appear, cresting the dunes like a mirage, shimmering in the heat rising up from the sand. They were all dressed in white. The women wore long dresses and I could see their legs through the material. The men led the way down to the water. One young man opened his shirt and it cupped out in the breeze like moth wings. Another boy stopped and rolled up his trousers, then ran to catch up with the group. A little girl with a flame of red hair did a cartwheel and got tangled in her dress so that she fell lopsided upside-down.

The crowd drew up by the water's edge and formed a loose circle. An old man with white hair, dressed in a white suit and holding a white book, stepped into the centre. He bowed his head and the rest followed his example, then he led them into the sea up to their waists so the children had to be carried. The old man stood apart from the group and summoned the young man who had opened his shirt on the way down. He stepped forward and the old man reached out and touched him on the top of his head. The young man sank into the water and rose up again when the hand was released. The women suddenly started to clap and sing, swaying from side to side. The young man, his hair flattened against his head, looked up at the sky as if waiting for something to happen. After a while, he shrugged and strode out of the ocean using his arms like scythes to part the water. The old man shouted after him but the young man didn't look back.

The women stopped singing and everybody stood still, watching the young man walk away. They looked like posts standing in the water, their white clothes filled with air and bobbing on the surface, the waves lapping against their bodies. A seagull swooped down and caught a fish in its beak, then ascended. After a moment, a blonde woman scurried after the young man. Then another man followed him out of the water, carrying a baby in his arms. Soon the whole crowd was rushing out of the ocean, crossing the sand and returning from where they had come.

I stood up and shaded my eyes and watched the last of the white figures disappear down the road, then slowly made my way to Peter's. When I got there, I explained to him what I'd seen. What was that all about? I asked him.

Beats me, he shrugged. Baptists probably. People come to the ocean for all sorts of reasons. Some people think it will cleanse them of their sins, but it doesn't always work that way. You've got to believe in all that mumbo-jumbo to begin with 'cause at the end of the day it's just a whole lot of water, he said, twisting the cap off a Thermos and pouring out a cup of coffee. He went into the boathouse and came out with a pair of steel rowlocks. Here you go, he said. You might as well have a matching pair, and handed them to me.

Thanks, I said and went round the back and got to work. It was nearly noon when I saw Anna coming down the beach towards me. We stood looking at each other for a little while and then we both began talking at once.

Look, she said. Maybe I should have told you . . .

I don't care about your epilepsy. It doesn't bother me.

Well it bothers me.

It shouldn't . . .

I wanted to tell you. I wanted to explain about my dad. He's really a wonderful person.

I'm sorry, I said. I was confused. I didn't know . . .

I know.

We stopped talking then and started to laugh. She kicked me and I grabbed her by the ribs and started to tickle her. She shrieked and ran down the beach. I sprinted after her and we collapsed in the sand, giggling and gasping for breath. We lay on our backs for a long time until the silence surrounded and enfolded us. Only the sound of the waves whispering along the shore. Those goddamn seagulls circling for food. Our breathing rose and fell in unison. Everything was in synch.

After a while I propped myself up on an elbow and said, So tell me about it. What's it like? How long have you had it?

Three years, she said, rolling onto her stomach. When my mother left us for this other guy, I knew she'd broken my father's heart, although you'd never know it by the way he talks. Sometimes I think he feels guiltier than he lets on. Doesn't show his true feelings. Not like me. I felt so betrayed, only I tried to resist it. As much as I could. I was twelve and I cried for a month and then my heart, or the part reserved for mother, simply turned to stone. It's like I have this rock inside me. It doesn't go away but I've learned to live with it. And when I saw her again, one whole year after she left us, all I felt was hardness. I hated her and the sight of her made this stone rise up in my mouth and I couldn't speak. I hit her. She's not big. I hit her right in the face, and I kept hitting her until my father pulled me off. I remember the blank look on her face, how she didn't fight back, only stood there and took it. Her nose was bleeding. I had my first attack soon after that. I've been having them ever since.

It's not so bad, she continued. I can't remember anything. I get a few warning signals. Everything becomes intensified. Colours get deeper, brighter. Noises get louder. I have a code with my dad. When I call him Baba, if I still can, then he knows I'm having an attack and if he's around, he whisks me off. He tries to be discreet. He'd rather people misunderstood him than knew about me because it's not pretty, John. It looks pretty horrible. I remember watching a film in Boston at the hospital of a girl having a fit. She bit her lip and there was blood. She was foaming at the mouth and her body was so distorted. I remember thinking I don't want anybody to see me like that. I made my dad promise he wouldn't let anybody see me like that.

I wouldn't mind, I said.

Well, I would.

Then I'd close my eyes.

You would not. You'd be too curious.

If you asked me to close my eyes, I would.

Close your eyes.

I closed my eyes. She kissed my mouth. She opened her lips and I felt her tongue skip across my teeth like a garter snake.

It's done! The boat is ready! I yelled, barging into Shirley's and yanking Anna by the arm. You've got to come.

But I haven't finished my sandwich yet.

Oh, forget it. Just leave it there. That's okay, Shirley, isn't it?

Sure, sure. Go on, Anna.

I dragged Anna out of the diner and we ran down to the beach. Peter was standing in the door of the boathouse smoking a cigarette. When he saw us coming, he kicked the door frame with the side of his foot and went inside.

I took Anna round the back and showed her my boat with a flourish and a da-dum. I bowed and she gave me a round of applause.

It's great, John. Painted and everything. It's beautiful.

Blue and white. Just like the boats in Greece. But there's one last thing to do. I've got to christen it. I want to name it after you. I've got some black paint and I want you to sign the boat, really big, on the prow, just like you would on a cheque, in cursive.

I've never signed a cheque before in my life.

So pretend. I'll go get the paint.

Anna knelt in the sand, tucked her hair behind her ears, dipped the brush into the paint and wiped it against the lip of the can until she had a good fine point then, chewing her bottom lip in concentration, signed her name. She leaned back and tilted her head and said, There. It's done. Anna.

Anna, I repeated to myself.

Well, John, Peter said, rounding the boathouse. I see you've done it. Did the pitch take? Get a good seal?

Far as I know, I said.

I'll check it later. But for now, congratulations, and he shook my hand. You're missing something, though.

What's that? I asked.

Well, with your nocturnal habits, you're going to need a light of some sort so the other boats can see you.

Peter produced a storm lamp from behind his back. A beautiful brass lamp with a little lever to raise the glass and a reservoir for oil and a wick like a shoe tongue sticking out, waiting to be lit.

Wow, I said. Thanks, Peter.

Well, don't just stand there. Light the damn thing, he said and took out a lighter and handed it to me. I lit it then lowered the glass bell and we stood around admiring the flame.

[79]

One last thing. You can't christen a boat without a bottle of champagne.

He went into the boathouse and came back with a bottle.

The cheapest kind of sparkling wine, he announced. Courtesy of Mick. Peter poured the stuff into three tin cups then handed me the bottle. You got to break it now. On the prow. Just throw it if you want.

I walked solemnly to the front and took a few steps sideways. I threw the bottle and it ricocheted off the edge and fell fully intact onto the sand. I stared at the bottle for a while then started to laugh. I laughed for a full few seconds then grew quiet. I looked at the bottle again and felt like it was mocking me. I grabbed it by the neck and, still holding it, brought it smashing down on the wooden side. The bottle shattered and cut my hand in two places. Peter went and got some peroxide and a couple of Band-Aids from his first aid kit. I sat down beside Anna and we watched the blood trickle out of the cuts. Peter fixed me up and we sat there for a minute, staring silently at the boat.

Peter raised his tin cup and said, To Anna, and we all drank the bitter fizzy wine. I looked at her, then at him, and I started to laugh again. We all began to laugh. We laughed until the wine was gone and then we drank some beer and kept laughing until our sides ached and the sun had set and the stars were giggling up in the heavens.

Peter made a fire on the beach, laid out a few old blankets and stayed with us until it was dark. He closed the boathouse door and locked it with a padlock. He hitched up his right pant leg and pushed his bike across the beach. The spokes caught the moonlight and blinked as the wheels skimmed across the surface. Anna and I sat quietly together, watching his shrinking silhouette.

Anna looked down at her hands. She was tracing spirals and star shapes in the sand. Her skin glowed orange in the light from the smouldering ashes, warm against the blackness behind her. I looked up and felt like I was sitting at the centre of an immense upside-down bowl. The boathouse was only a shade paler than the night sky and appeared as flat and unreal as a stage prop. I can remember everything exactly the way it was. I knew how I felt about Anna. I knew how I would always feel about her and I wanted to do something about it. I knew we had our entire lives ahead of us but I wanted to make that moment last forever.

I turned to her and said, Anna, will you marry me?

Marry you?

Not now, I said. When we're older.

Maybe, she said.

We could build a house up in the woods.

And have children, she said. Do you want to have kids, John?

I dunno. I never really thought about it.

I could write books, just like my dad. He could live with us.

And I'd have a scuba-diving business.

We could open up a restaurant. My dad could cook. He's always talked about opening a restaurant.

We could call it the Seahorse Restaurant, I said.

The Seahorse, she repeated. Ya, that's nice. I like that.

And I could bring you the fish I caught. And lobsters and crabs and oysters.

Have you ever had an oyster?

No, I said. Have you?

Once, she said. I didn't like it very much. It's supposed to be an aphrodisiac.

A what? I asked.

Something that turns you on.

Sexually, you mean?

Ya, sexually.

Are you turned on?

Kinda. Are you?

Ya, I said and turned away. My palms felt sweaty. My heart was thumping inside my chest, making my t-shirt flutter. Do you wanna do it?

Do what? she asked.

You know, I said. Now that we're engaged.

But I haven't said yes, yet.

Please say yes.

Do you think we're ready for this? she asked.

Do you?

I've never done it before.

Neither have I.

I've been saving myself, she said.

What for? I asked.

Till I got married, I guess.

But we're gonna get married, I said. I can feel it. I'm sure of it.

But it's gotta be just right, she said.

It will be.

And romantic, she said.

This *is* romantic.

You better not be leading me on.

I'm not, I said. I love you, Anna.

Do you really?

Cross my heart and hope to die.

Then let's do it. Right here. Under the stars.

Anna . . .

What?

I don't know what to do.

I'll show you, she said and leaned over and kissed me.

We lay back on a blanket and I wrapped my arms around her and pulled her towards me. I felt her breasts under her t-shirt, soft and firm as dough-balls. Her nipples like raisins between my fingers. I felt her breath quicken. Her face was in shadow. I looked into her eyes and saw a dark forest. When it was time, she showed me how. I let her lead me. She pulled me deep into the woods.

It's not something I can really describe although it was kind of like diving into the ocean at night. I broke the surface and she swallowed me up. It was something like that only there was a serious element to it too. Something sad about the way it came and went and the way I felt empty afterwards, only I knew we'd tied some knots at the same time. The human heart is made of string. I am still attached to her by a single thread. I've been letting it out ever since like there's an infinite supply on my spool for her. No matter where I am, I can always find my way back.

When it was over, she raised herself on one elbow and reached down between her legs. She drew her hand up to my face. She held a little slug of blood between her thumb and forefinger. I took her finger and put it in my mouth. I saw the embers burning in her eyes. I kissed each eyelid and whispered, Always.

Then I said, Forever.

It was a windless night. The air was warm and maternal. A three-quarter moon hung in the sky and bats occasionally darted from the boathouse into the black sky and back again, their presence signalled only by the sound of air splitting.

Anna sat up. So whaddya wanna do now? she asked.

I wanna go for a swim.

Ya, but I can't.

I know, but it would feel so good.

I wish I could watch you dive.

Why don't you come up to the point with me?

No, she said. I don't wanna be left up there all by myself.

Anna paused. She looked out at the glassy water vibrating with a million stars on its back. She looked back at the boathouse, at my rowboat, then at me.

I could take the boat out and watch you dive from out there, she said, pulling on her clothes. Come on, how hard could it be? Help me get it into the water.

I'll swim out and meet you, then I can row us back to shore. Here take that end.

We dragged the boat into the water and I ran back for the oars. I inserted them into the rowlocks and sat down on the bench.

You just hold them like this and pull back. Try to make sure the tips stay in the water. If you want to go right pull harder on the left.

You sit backwards?

[84]

Ya.

So how do you see where you're going?

You look over your shoulder. Tide's going out, so you'll get some help from the current, but it's not that far. Maybe a hundred feet till you can see around the point. I'll be waiting for you.

I watched her wade into the water. She gripped the side of the boat and slid into the middle of the bench.

Wait a minute! I yelled and ran back to get the storm lamp. I lit it and wedged it into the triangle at the prow of the boat so that it shone before her. Anna took the oars and I pushed her out. She smiled and I turned and ran up the beach and onto the path. I flew up the rocks in record time, barely feeling the sharp edges under my feet, timing my jumps and grabbing all the familiar hand-holds. I stood there in my shorts, feeling the breeze on my thighs and the small of my back. I stretched and felt the muscle go taut across my ribs. I waited for Anna to appear and then, like a firefly, I saw her inching her way across the water. The lamplight reflected off the glassy surface, surrounding the boat in a hundred floating candles.

Up here! I called out and waved both arms over my head.

Anna lifted her hand to wave back and the oar began to slip through the rowlock. She lurched to retrieve it and the lamp fell over and all the flickering candles vanished off the surface. Anna waited until the boat was steady. She repositioned the oar and started to row again and I saw a flame dart up behind her. Anna! I screamed. Behind you! But she didn't hear me. A tongue of fire licked the prow and curled up over the gunnel. The flame ignited along a seam of fresh pitch and ran the length of the inside hull. The sinew shot past Anna and she jumped up, wobbling the boat. She stood with her legs spread for balance, holding her arms out while both oars slipped into the water.

John! she screamed. Help me!

There was an explosion where the oil lamp was and the bow burst into flames. Anna stood stock-still as the fire spread out behind her, her silhouette black against a background of white flames. The fire was spreading along each new ribbon of pitch, between every moulded plank, encircling her in burning hoola-hoops.

I'm coming! I shouted and flew off the cliff. The waves offered little resistance and I seemed to surface in one powerful kick of my legs. I whipped the hair out of my eyes and looked over at the boat. The whole thing was burning but I couldn't see Anna anywhere. She wasn't in the boat. It was drifting out with the tide and I had to swim hard to catch up with it. At first I did the crawl, without putting my face in the water because I didn't want to take my eyes off it, but I was going too slowly so I put my head down and swam as fast as I could, and as I got closer I could see the glowing halo of the flames underwater. When I reached the boat, I heard a crack and part of the hull buckled and snapped off and drifted away. I could hear flames hissing as the boat began to sink.

Anna! I shouted. Answer me!

I looked around in every direction. The ocean was too still, too calm. Empty except for the smouldering carcass of my boat sizzling on the water. I dove down blindly, searching with my hands. I kept descending until the pressure nearly burst my eardrums. I scrambled to the top and gasped for breath. I felt something nudge my shoulder and spun around and grabbed onto an oar floating aimlessly through the water. I kicked the air and headed back into the depths. I went down far enough to feel the temperature drop.

There was nothing but the weight of the water closing in on my body and the gurgling sound of the sea like blood being pumped through a heart. I felt something brush against my leg and doubled back. I paddled up. I took another breath and headed down again. Every dive became harder. I began to fear the dark and the soundlessness. It held a horror for me that I had never known before. I wanted to stay on the surface, tread water, breathe air, but I forced myself to go in deeper.

When I surfaced, my eyes were hot and I knew that I was crying. I fought the contractions of my lungs and plunged back down. I kept diving until I tasted blood in my mouth. I thought of the blood between her fingers. Her shiny black hair all covered in seaweed. The Band-Aids on her knees. The way she cracked her gum. Anna! I shouted to the air. I put my face into the water and shouted again. I hit the ocean with my fists. I wrestled with it.

When I was completely exhausted, I floated on my back until I felt strong enough to dive again. I stayed in the water until the sun rose and the tide had turned, urging me ashore. I didn't fight it and, as the ocean turned from black to blue, I dragged myself onto the beach and fell asleep.

The coast guard found her body three days later near Santa Cruz. A couple of kids found her near the boardwalk, not far from the fairgrounds and the ecstatic screams coming off the loop-de-loop, washed up with Coke cans and the cardboard centres of cotton candy. She would have had her cutoffs on and a soggy pack of Marlboros in her back pocket. Raw, white patches on her knees where the Band-Aids had soaked off.

Her death was pronounced accidental.

From a distance, hidden behind a tree, I watched Nick pack his car, then carry boxes into a U-haul trailer. He worked slowly and methodically all afternoon, placing one foot in front of the other, back and forth from the house more than thirty times, until the air lost its warmth and gradually the light softened into pink. A light in the kitchen went on and I watched him fill the kettle by the sink in front of the window. He looked up and let the water run.

I returned later that night and crept up the stairs and onto the porch. I peered in through the window. Nick was sitting on a milk crate in front of a makeshift table. He was writing something down on a piece of paper. Suddenly, he sighed and put his pen down. He dropped his head into his hands and wept. After a while, he looked up again and licked his lips. He smoothed his hair and wiped his eyes, then rubbed the back of his neck. He cleared his throat and picked up his pen and started to write again.

Part Two

I was driving with the windows down, sun behind me making a long shadow of the car on the road ahead like I was chasing a ghost I could never quite catch. White knuckles on the steering wheel. I had to make an effort to relax my grip, like if I could hold onto the wheel of the car tight enough I could prevent my life from spinning out of control. My fingers were stained with nicotine. I looked at my face in the rearview mirror. Eighteen years old, but I felt fifty. My lungs were shot. Couldn't have held my breath for more than twenty seconds. I downshifted into third and stepped on the gas, overtaking a sixteen-wheeler, and popped back into the middle lane. Cruised along in fourth. The wind was playing with my hair. Felt good. I took a drag and flicked my cigarette out the window. I switched on the radio and Lou Reed was straining across the wire. I turned up the volume and hung my arm across the top of the steering wheel.

I tried to concentrate on the driving. Due south on the Interstate, about three hours north of LA. I wanted to get out of California but I wanted to drive east through the southern states. I had need of some wide open space and the desert seemed to be calling me. I'd had enough of the ocean for the time being.

My life had taken a nose dive after I left Round Bay. Ran away to San Francisco when I turned sixteen. Spent two weeks getting high with the deadheads in Golden Gate Park, drinking cider with the bums and panhandling on the Haight for a dime or a dollar. It didn't take me long to get in with a crowd of street kids. Everyone had their own reasons for not being at home or in school, no matter how great or small the abuse they were running away from. After a few weeks, I was invited to live in a co-op by a guy I'd dropped acid with. I did everything I could to forget where I had come from, but the only thing I managed to forget was time, and two whole years went by without my noticing. Finally, I decided I'd had enough. I had to get out. That house was like a black hole sucking in all the garbage of the world.

I got a loan of a couple of sheets of acid from a friend and started selling on the street in order to save up enough money to buy a secondhand car. When I was about twelve hundred dollars in the clear, I found an old Dodge Omni for three hundred bucks, chose New York City as my destination and, on June 30th, 1988, got into my car and left for good. I wanted to put as much distance as I could between me and my past, and figured New York was as far east as I could go without driving right into the ocean on the other side.

I'd been driving for about five hours when I saw a girl hitchhiking on the road ahead of me. She had long hair, dark and shiny in the late sun. The shadow of her body stretched across the highway and slid over the top of my car as I went by. She was wearing a t-shirt and a pair of jeans. She couldn't have been going far because she didn't have any luggage, no backpack or anything, and although I didn't slow down I kept on thinking about her. It's not often you see a woman hitchhiking alone. If you do, she's either trouble or just plain stupid. Still, she left some sort of impression and I couldn't help thinking about her.

I turned off the radio. I listened to the sound of the wind in my ear like a busted pipe. The sun was setting. The sky to my right was tangerine and laced with pink, all scarlet around the white disc of the sun. The fields were gold and green velvet patches. I like that time of evening. The light is special and lingers for a while before it disappears. Colours are more intense. Greens seem greener. Stars come out although the sky's still light. California is beautiful. I miss it. But there wasn't much left there for me anymore. I hadn't spoken to my dad for two years, not once during the whole time I was in San Francisco.

When I told him I was planning to leave Round Bay, he asked me where I thought I was going to go. I told him San Francisco and he nodded and said good luck, and then he took a cold beer out of the fridge and went into the living-room and switched on the TV and that was the end of the discussion. He didn't try to stop me and didn't even say goodbye, even when I started to pack right under his nose. I guess he felt there wasn't much he could do. Maybe he was too tired to try or maybe he just didn't give a shit. Whatever the case, I still wonder how he's doing sometimes, whether he's okay or if he's moved. He must be feeling his age. Never did take good care of himself. Guess he's lonely. So am I.

I was hungry so I decided to stop at the next rest stop and get a coffee and something to eat. I signalled off into the exit lane and slowed down. I parked in a far corner of the lot and walked into the service station. There was a Dunkin' Donuts on the left and a Burger King counter to my right. I went over to the Burger King and ordered a Whopper, large fries, large coffee and an apple turnover. The girl behind the counter had her hair trapped in a hair net. She was pretty curt, although she fed me all the regulation lines like, Have a nice day, sir. She couldn't have been much younger than me and I was tempted to ask her if she wanted to go on a road trip, but on closer inspection, she wasn't all that pretty and would have probably stunk the car up with french-fry grease. I took my tray over to a table in the smoking section and sat down.

Across from me an old woman bit into a hamburger and some white sauce dribbled down her chin. She didn't wipe it off or anything and the sight of it made me sad and sick. I decided to take my meal out to the car and sit on the hood where the air was fresh and I could watch the sky. I propped my feet up on the bumper and rested my elbows on my knees. I ate quickly so I could have a smoke.

As I was sitting there, a patrol car drove by slowly. I could hear the static and the messages coming over the police radio. I watched as the car turned into my lane. The cop in the passenger seat looked at me and I gave him a nod. He nodded back and they drove on. I got off the hood, opened the front door of the car and sat sideways in the seat with my feet on the ground. I reached back and picked up a bottle of Tequila that was on the floor and took a deep swig. The alcohol did its job and a warm feeling spread from the base of my skull down my spine. I took another drink, capped the bottle and threw it back onto the floor.

I started the car and pulled out of the rest stop. It was pretty dark by then, almost night, and on my way down the merge lane the same girl I saw before was standing on the side of the road holding her thumb out and waiting for a lift. I slowed down then pulled over. I watched her run towards the car in the rearview mirror. She came up and opened the door.

Hi. Where you going? she asked.

East, I said.

She paused for a moment and then she said, You know you're going south.

Yep.

But you're heading east eventually.

That's right.

How far you going?

All the way.

How far's all the way.

New York City, I said.

Really? That's where I'm headed. Can I get a lift?

To New York?

Ya, she said.

Where are your things? I asked her.

Haven't got any.

Whaddya mean?

It's a long story.

Are you a runaway?

No. I'm going home.

New York?

Montreal, actually. But New York'll do.

You Canadian?

Ya, she said, ducking her head further inside the car.

I looked out of my window for a moment and then turned to her and said, I don't know if I can take you the whole way . . .

Whatever, she said, getting in and slamming the door. She

turned to me and smiled. Thanks, she said, I'll go as far as you want. If you want to get rid of me at any point, just say the word, and it's okay by me.

She took out a pack of Marlboros and lit a cigarette. She exhaled and her smoke smacked into the windshield like a car crash in slow-mo, spread out and curled down over the dashboard.

Ready when you are, she said, raising an eyebrow. I quickly put in the clutch, checked my blind spot and pulled onto the merge lane. When we had gained some speed and were on the road again, she leant back in her seat and let out a long deflating sigh, as if she'd been waiting a long time to do that.

The road was black except for the red tail-lights of the cars in front and the bright beams of oncoming traffic. I turned to look at her. The headlights from a car travelled briefly over her face and her profile was fine and fragile in the dark.

I smell booze, she said. Have you got any?

Some Tequila, I said. It's on the floor.

I felt her arm brush against my leg as she bent down to retrieve the bottle under my feet. She took a drink and smacked her lips.

Ah, Tequila, she said and wound the window up. She leaned into the corner between the seat and the door and handed me the bottle. We drove on for another twenty minutes before I noticed that she had fallen asleep. I reached over and turned the volume way down, then switched on the radio. I made sure it wasn't loud enough to wake her and tuned into some jazz station. The music was melancholy and I felt cozy in the orange glow of the instrument panel, with the air coming in balmy through the window and this girl asleep by my side. I barely noticed the DJ introduce song after song because they all sounded the same to me, like the drone of the tires on the smooth pavement. I fell into the rhythm of driving, lured by the red demon eyes of the cars in front, winding across an invisible countryside in my little Dodge Omni.

It's so dark out here, she said suddenly and I nearly jumped out of my skin.

You were asleep, I said.

How long? she asked.

I dunno.

What time is it?

Around midnight?

Where are we?

We've skirted around LA. Still going south.

We must be in the mountains. It's cooler up here. I can smell sage.

Ya. Smells good, I said and strained to see, beyond the headlights, the dark sloping sides of the hills, the rocks rising up on either side like cardboard cutouts, black against a sky now dotted with stars.

My mouth is parched. Got any more Tequila?

It's all gone. I'll stop at the next place we come to.

Thanks.

You got any money?

Yeah, she said sharply and turned to look out the window and ended up staring herself in the face. I turned the radio up and she pulled her knees up to her chest.

We were on the Interstate heading east towards Arizona.

The road curved and we came out onto a straightaway with a gas station up ahead, some neon motel signs, a diner and a bar called the Redwood Tavern. I pulled into the gas station and turned off the engine. I looked at the girl and saw her face clearly for the first time under the fluorescent light. She had the kind of face that's more beautiful the more haggard it gets. Her skin was tanned, but she had dark circles under her eyes. Her mouth was small but deep red, almost brown, and her hands were folded in her lap like an obedient schoolgirl, except that she had rings on most of her fingers. When she noticed me looking at her hands she fidgeted and started scraping the dirt from under her fingernails.

I took the keys from the ignition and got out of the car. I unhooked the pump and unscrewed the gas cap. I inserted the nozzle and pulled the trigger and felt the gas rush into the tank without once taking my eyes off the back of her head. The smell wafted up and made me dizzy. I knocked the metal nozzle a few times to get the last drops out and put it back. She hadn't moved so I walked over to the attendant and paid. He told me it was thirty minutes past twelve.

Bar still open? I asked him.

Should be, he said and handed me a receipt.

When I got back to the car, I asked her if she wanted to go for a drink.

Ya, she said. I'd love to, so I drove across the lot and parked outside the tavern. We both got out and walked over to the bar. I could hear the unmistakable twang of Country and Western. The place was dark and smoky and surprisingly crowded for a Thursday night. There was a small dance floor in the middle of the room, thick wooden tables and chairs, and a bar running the length of the far wall which was lined with bottles all back-lit and full of amber liquid shining like jewels in a glass case. There was a pool table in the corner with a light hanging down over the centre so the green felt stood out like a football field at night. Some people turned to look at us as we walked in, but most of them just carried on drinking and talking.

Couples were spinning on the floor and some of the men were wearing cowboy hats. The dance floor was marked off by six thick, circular pillars, shiny brown, uneven in parts, with dark knots here and there on the surface. My eyes followed the pillars to the ceiling and I realized they were upturned tree trunks with the roots still intact, polished and varnished. The roots spread out and ran along the ceiling like we were underground in a rabbit warren or a badger's den.

I'm gonna go to the bathroom, she said, so I went over to the bar and ordered a Bud. I carried my beer to a table and sat down. After a while, I saw her come out of the bathroom and head over to the bar where a man was standing alone. She smiled at him and struck up a conversation. After a while, the man leaned in closer, threw his head back and laughed. He raised two fingers to the bartender and she brought over two bottles of beer. It made me angry. There I was, offering to take this girl all the way to New York and she didn't even have the decency to sit with me and have a drink. I finished my beer and walked over to the bar. When she saw me coming, she interrupted the man to introduce me.

This is my friend . . . ah. We're travelling together, she said.

The man nodded.

Hi there, I said and felt his eyes travel down my body and

back up hers. He was built like a brick shithouse and didn't seem too thrilled about my presence, so I said, I think we should be going.

Don't you want another one? she asked.

If you're buying, I said.

Well, maybe we should stick to our itinerary. See ya round, she said and headed for the door. I apologized to the man and turned and followed her out.

When I got out to the parking lot, she was lighting a cigarette.

Nice one, I said.

Whaddya mean?

Trying to get me killed?

Aw, come on, she said. He was harmless.

To you, maybe.

Look, he just bought me a drink, that's all.

I know. I saw.

You got a problem with that?

Only when it involves me.

Well, it didn't, okay?

It could've, I said.

You didn't have to come over, she said.

Oh, you're right, I said. I should've just sat in my corner till you'd had your fun and were ready to leave. What am I? Your fucken chauffeur?

Look, you don't have to take me any further than this, you know.

And what, just leave you here?

If you want.

And what would you do then?

Look, I can take care of myself. I've done it so far just fine on my own. I don't need your help.

If you don't want to come with me, that's fine.

I didn't say that. I just don't belong to you, that's all.

I never fucken said you did.

I'm just not allowed to talk to other guys, is that it?

What the fuck are you talking about? I just thought you might have had the courtesy to join me for a drink, that's all.

She took another drag and dropped her butt onto the gravel and crushed it with her shoe.

He wasn't gonna beat you up, she said.

How do you know that?

I wouldn't have let him.

I would have liked to have seen that, I said and laughed.

He was a big softy, she said.

He was a Neanderthal.

He told me he had a daughter about my age. I think he was just being paternal, that's all.

I rubbed my eyes with the heel of my hand and said, Look, you comin' or not because I wanna get back on the road.

'Course I'm comin', she said. It's gonna be harder than that to get rid of me.

Well, I just hope it doesn't involve getting the shit kicked outta me.

I'll try not to let that happen.

After I'd started the car and was about to pull out, she turned to me and said, My name is Hannah. Hannah Crowe and I'm seventeen years old. Last January I took a Greyhound bus from Montreal to San Francisco with two hundred bucks in my pocket. I've been living on the street for six months and it's time to go home. I didn't sit down with you because I didn't want you to know that I have no money. So now you know.

Why Hannah? I asked.

Whaddya mean?

Why are you called Hannah?

I dunno, she said. Apparently, or this is my mother's version of the story, my Rumanian grandmother looked into my crib at the hospital when I was born and said that I was going to have everything she never had as a child. That I was going to live the life she'd missed out on. So my mother named me after her and then she died, which was probably for the best because I'm sure she'd be disappointed if she could see me now. Sometimes I think she can and it gives me this creepy feeling, like I'm some sort of a bad seed.

Your mother died? I asked.

No, my grandmother. Her name was Hannah.

Ya, I got that part, I said and pulled out of the parking lot.

So what's yours? she asked.

John, I said. John Wade.

Pleased to meet you, John.

Likewise.

We drove till dawn and straight into sunrise. The sky grew lighter. The stars disappeared. A thin strip of pale yellow flooded the horizon and the sun rose white into an almost white sky. We stopped at a greasy spoon and ate bacon and eggs. The waitress brought the bill and we sat smoking cigarettes and drinking coffee. Hannah emptied out a pack of sugar onto the table and started tracing patterns with her finger.

So how come you haven't got any stuff with you? I asked her.

Got stolen.

Everything?

My backpack. Sleeping bag.

How'd it happen?

At a truck stop. I was hitchhiking down Highway 1 and got dropped at a truck stop. They don't like to serve hitch-hikers in the diners there, so I put my backpack in a field just beside the parking lot and went in for breakfast. When I came out, everything was gone, and I know it sounds unbelievable but there was this big, shiny black sixteen-wheeler parked on the edge of the field when I went in and it was gone when I came out. I'm sure it was him. Big fucken semi. Like Darth Vader on wheels. So there I was. Nothing but the clothes on my back. And you know what? It was kind of liberating. I felt free. No responsibilities. I owned nothing and belonged to no one.

And you haven't had any money since then?

Not really . . . Sorry.

Why are you apologizing?

Well, would you have given me a lift? I mean, if I had said, Hi, I'm completely broke and I want a lift all the way to New York, would you have said, Sure babe, hop in? I bet you would have said, Fuck that, see ya later.

Maybe not.

Well, I didn't want to risk it. Besides I didn't want to give you the wrong idea either.

What's that supposed to mean?

You know. Typical scenario. Girl's broke. Guy's got something girl wants. Girl's got something guy wants. I dunno. It was late. I was tired. That's the worst, being tired on the road, because everything that's normally easy to cope with starts feeling impossible. Just the darkness alone seems threatening.

You mean, you thought I might think you were a hooker?

Not exactly, but some guys think that if they buy you dinner then you owe them something. That they have a right to fuck you, as if you had a price tag on your forehead. I just didn't know if you were like that or not.

Well, I'm not, I said.

Phew, that's a relief, she said, smiling and pretending to wipe the sweat off her brow.

What's so funny?

You just didn't have to say that, that's all.

Why not?

Well, I've already figured out that you're not like that.

You never know.

True. You could still turn out to be an axe murderer, but you seem like a pretty nice guy.

Oh, I said.

Well, aren't you?

Well, I don't think I've ever hurt anyone intentionally. Not that I can think of.

Most people don't.

Don't what?

Hurt people intentionally.

No?

I don't think so. They do it by accident, or because they're stupid.

Ya, but it's still their fault.

To an extent, she said. I'd hate to think I was to blame for everything bad I've ever done. Anyway, if I ever hurt anybody, it's usually myself so it's not like I ever get away with it. Still, it's easier to accept hurting yourself than somebody else, I think. It certainly seems easier to do, more likely, you know?

Like what?

Like thinking that a guy who's just bought me dinner has the right to sleep with me.

But that's ridiculous. You just said so yourself.

I know. I know. I don't know why I don't just tell them to fuck off. Maybe it has something to do with not respecting myself, or being afraid to say no. I've done a lot of damage to myself. Nothing irreparable, so that's a relief, but the thing is, and this is the point I'm trying to make, I could hate myself for having done those things, which would just make me do it more, out of self-hatred, or I could forgive myself by saying that what I've done in the past I've done by accident or out of my own stupidity. If I can forgive myself, then I can change. There's room for improvement. Blaming yourself doesn't help. Are you following me?

Not really, I said. How old did you say you were? Seventeen?

Girls mature faster than boys. Up to the age of twenty or so, girls are normally two years more mature than boys.

Is that a fact.

Whatever, she said. I still think they have a better understanding of themselves. They have to. They're forced to think about themselves more because they find themselves in situations men don't.

Like what?

Well, for instance, you've just accepted a meal and a lift from this truck driver, and you're at some rest stop in the middle of nowhere, and he starts putting his hands down your pants. What do you do? It might even feel good up to a point. But past that point? What do you do? Tell him to go to hell? Piss him off? Run away? On one hand, you feel responsible. On the other hand, you feel trapped. If he got angry, he could really hurt you. Hurt you worse than if you just close your eyes and grit your teeth and bare it.

This ever happen to you?

Sure, she said. With my lifestyle . . .

I'm sorry to hear that, I said.

Not as sorry as I am.

It's not a competition, I said. I'm just saying . . .

You're right. It's a bad thing. And the worst part about it is that it all boils down to money.

It's a fucken drag, I said.

Tell me about it, she said.

We sat there for a while, staring into our empty coffee mugs.

You shouldn't hitchhike, I said eventually.

I think I'm a pretty good judge of character. The majority of people are good. I believe that. I've met some wonderful people . . .

But they can't all be good.

I know, she said. Knock on wood.

Look, I said. I'll take you all the way to New York.

Really?

Ya.

Are you sure?

Ya.

Thanks, John. I really appreciate it.

I ground my cigarette into the ashtray and stretched my arms over my head. My eyes were heavy with sleep and the colours inside the diner looked acidic. I'm exhausted, I said. I'm gonna have to stop soon.

I don't have a license, she said, but I can drive if you want me to.

Maybe when we hit the desert.

So we're going through the desert?

Ya, I said. New Mexico, Texas. I've never been. Thought I'd see it now while I have the chance.

I took out enough money from my wallet to cover the bill and a tip.

Thanks for breakfast, she said.

Don't mention it.

Why are you doing this for me? she asked.

I dunno. I like the company, I guess.

I'll make it up to you, John.

Please don't say that.

Ya, but . . . she said, glancing down at the table.

It's only money.

Still . . .

It was the first of July and another hot day. The sun was glinting off the windshield making the glass look milky. I took off my jean jacket and threw it on the back seat. I didn't own much when I left San Francisco. All I took were the clothes on my back and what was left of the money I'd saved up after buying the car, just under nine hundred dollars, enough to get me to New York. But now I had Hannah to think about. An extra expense.

God, it's hot, she said and hung her head out the window. The car smelt faintly of sweat and it must have been hers, because I didn't think I could notice my own. I looked over at the strip of waist above her hip where her t-shirt had lifted away from her jeans. The skin was pale and tight and curved forward around her stomach. I followed the line of her ass down to her thighs and felt a pulse in my crotch, felt myself go hard. She took something out of her pocket, like a strip from a handkerchief and tied up her hair. I blinked at the heat rising in waves off the tarmac and tried to concentrate on the driving.

I'm really thirsty, she said.

Ya, it's pretty dry, eh?

Eh?

What?

You sounded Canadian there.

Well, technically I am.

Really? Where you from?

Bella Coola. It's in northern BC.

How long have you been in the States?

Too long.

No, really.

My dad and I moved here when I was eight. After my mother left.

Where'd she go?

I dunno. Ran off with an Indian.

Really?

Honest to God.

Ever see her?

No, not since then. I'd have no idea where to start looking.

Oh, she said.

It's alright. Can't miss what you never had.

That's not true. We all want things we've never had.

I suppose. How about you? Got any parents?

Ya, two. The original ones. I haven't spoken to them since I left. I feel kinda bad about that.

They must be going crazy.

I know. I know.

You should call them at least. When we stop. Call them collect.

I couldn't.

Why not?

Aw, I dunno. I feel kinda guilty. I mean, they're not bad people. Just close-minded. We're very different.

Fuck that, man. They must be going outta their minds.

I don't know about that. Sometimes I think they must feel relieved.

But they don't even know where you are.

I've sent them a few postcards. Wish you were here, that sorta thing.

But I'm sure they'd want to hear your voice.

Let's just change the subject, okay?

No. This is really important.

Well, tell me about your dad then?

He gave me his blessing when I left. I'm sure he doesn't miss me.

See? There you go. Why should mine care and not yours?

It's different.

Why?

Well, I'm a guy, for one. Parents don't tend to worry so much about boys.

I can't believe you think that.

Well, it's true, isn't it? Besides, I happen to know for a fact that all I do is remind my dad of how miserable he is. He used to stare at me with this look on his face. Like he was looking right through me. It wasn't me he was seeing, you know. It was my mother. And God, you shoulda seen it. Such a sad look. Made me wanna cry. Sometimes it was spiteful too, like he hated the very core of me, or her, whoever it was he was looking at when he looked at me.

When was the last time you saw him?

Two years ago?

I think you should call him, too.

No way.

I'll call mine if you call yours.

Oh, that's tempting.

I'm being serious.

I'll think about it, I said. But I'm not making any promises.

The steering wheel felt greasy in my hands and my skin was prickly with heat. My muscles ached and my eyes were so tired that I was seeing things flatly, the way a dog sees things. Everything was two-dimensional. It was late afternoon and I was hungry, so we pulled into a gas station with a 7-Eleven and I told Hannah that I'd go get some food and booze and cigarettes. She said she'd come in with me but, before getting out of the car, she reached over the seat and picked up my jean jacket and put it on.

Nice jacket, she said, brushing past me into the store. I couldn't make her out. I didn't know whether to trust her or not. I couldn't tell what was going through her mind. She was like an old friend I'd never really gotten to know. Familiar and yet totally foreign. We roved up and down the aisles, slowly filling our arms with stuff, then lined up at the cash next to a display of fireworks.

Fourth of July, I said. We used to get those in Round Bay. Set them off on the beach. Watch them explode over the water.

Why don't you buy some? she asked.

Nah, I said and turned to face the counter. When it was my turn, I asked the guy for three packs of Marlboros and some matches.

See those maps? Hannah said, winking at me. Those are the ones I was telling you about.

I looked first at her, then at this rack of maps she was pointing to hanging on the back wall behind the counter.

Do you have one for South Dakota? she asked the cashier, an overweight teenager with a bad complexion. He had a giant Slurpy on the counter beside the register, the gallon kind, and his teeth were dyed a bright blue, the colour of Jaw Breakers. He swivelled round and started slowly flipping through the road maps.

No, don't think so, he said. Got one here for the whole States.

No, she said. That's not what I want. Never mind.

I paid the bill and we left the store. When we got into the car, I asked her what that was all about and she pulled three chocolate bars from my jean jacket pocket. Two Oh Henrys and a Mars bar. I thought she had something else up her sleeve because of the way she took off my jacket and placed it carefully on the back seat, but I didn't pry. We got back onto the Interstate and crossed the border into New Mexico. We continued driving until the sky in the west began to bleed, turned south towards El Paso and hit Texas by sundown. We drank beer and smoked cigarettes. We didn't talk much and listened to the radio. By the time it was dark, I was delirious for sleep.

I pulled into a rest area near the Devil Ridge Mountains and parked the car in a secluded corner by a picnic table and a fire pit. I longed for a shower, a bed and clean sheets, an evening spent in front of the TV. I thought how nice it would be to have a steak right now, something really solid in my stomach, and that was the last thing I thought before I fell asleep, slouched in the corner of the driver's seat.

I woke to the sound of a police siren, what I thought was a police siren, a high-pitched whistle then a bang, and a bright white flash of light. I sat bolt upright in my seat and grabbed the door handle. I jumped out of the car. It was dark and I could see Hannah standing on the grass in her bare feet beside the picnic table. Gold dust was showering down all around her, landing on her hair and shoulders like burning ash.

Surprise! she yelled, throwing her arms wide open.

I leaned back against the car with a hand on my heart. A couple of children from a nearby van came running over, screaming, Again! Again! Whoopee! Fireworks! Come on, mom! Come on, dad!

Hannah smiled and told them to stand back and twisted another Roman candle into the ground. She cupped her lighter around the wick and it went off like the fuse on a stick of dynamite. She took a few steps backwards and there was a pop, silence, then the sound of a gun shot overhead and a bright green waterfall of sparks. I sat down on the hood of the car. A few more people had left their cars and come over to watch. A gangly young girl stood off to one side and stared at Hannah. She had long blonde hair and when she saw me looking at her, dropped her head and shuffled her feet and scratched at a scab on her elbow. The parents of the two small children came round from behind the van. The husband was tall and dark-haired. He was holding a baby in his arms. His wife was plump and fair. She was holding him around the waist and walking slightly behind him, smiling and making cooing noises at the baby.

They walked over to me and asked, Having a little pre-fourth of July celebration? I think your girlfriend has made some friends.

I don't know if they've ever seen fireworks before, Jim, the wife said to her husband. Is it safe?

She looks like she knows what she's doing, Jim said, watching Hannah shoo the kids away and light another one. The wick fizzled out like a dying sparkler and there was a murmur of disappointment, then a series of excited oohs and aahs as the firework sputtered back to life, spewing out fountains of red, white and blue glitter. As the crowd was applauding, the cylinder gradually tilted and fell over onto the grass. It gained momentum and started spinning on the spot like a dog chasing its own tail, shooting sparks out sideways along the ground. Hannah jumped onto the picnic table and Jim shouted to his wife to get the kids. She ran to scoop them up, one under each arm like logs. Jim turned to me and handed me the baby, then rushed over and kicked the firework onto the gravel and stamped it out. There was an awkward pause while everybody stared at the charred tube. People began heading back to their vehicles and the baby started to cry. I looked down at its crumpled face and bounced it up and down in my arms. I held it by the armpits and bobbed it gently in the air.

When Jim was satisfied that the firework was safely extinguished and had dropped it in a metal garbage can, he came over, took the baby and said, You two are really damn lucky nobody got hurt.

I looked over at Hannah who was now sitting on the table with her chin resting in her hands. I walked over and asked if she was alright.

I'm fine, she said, refusing to look at me.

You sure? I said, a bit more softly.

Ya, she said and shrugged. It was just for fun. I thought you'd like it.

I did like it, I said. Especially the last one.

Oh, shut up, she said, swatting me on the arm.

Don't worry about them, I said.

I'm not worried about them, she said. I'm worried about you. I'm so embarrassed. You must think I'm totally stupid.

Why would I think that?

She gave me a look.

Let's just forget it, okay? We'll find a really secluded place and you can light the rest of them.

That was my last one, she said.

Well, at least it went out with a bang, I said, and Hannah said, Ha, ha, ha, and shoved me sideways as we headed back to the car.

When I woke up the next morning, my head was in Hannah's lap and she was looking down at me. It was early morning and the birds were going crazy. There was a thin film of dew on the windshield, evaporating in the quickly rising heat. I sat up and rubbed my eyes. I opened the door and placed my feet on the ground. The whole world was steaming. Mist was rising through the beams of light slanting through the trees. The grass was covered in diamonds. My body was stiff. It was Saturday morning, the second of July, and the rest stop was crowded with cars and camper-vans loaded down for the long holiday weekend.

Do you want me to drive? she asked.

I need a cup of coffee first, I said, ignoring the question.

There's a machine over there.

Let's drive somewhere.

Just for a change?

I looked at her and she was trying to suppress a grin. I couldn't help but smile.

Ya, that's right, I said.

As we were leaving the rest stop, we passed a pair of pay-phones and I pulled over. Why don't you give your folks a call? I said.

Only if you do, she said.

Why not.

I got out of the car and walked over to one of the booths

[115]

and folded back the door and stepped inside. I picked up the receiver and was suddenly filled with apprehension. What if my dad was drunk? Didn't know who I was? What if he ordered me to come home? I looked to my right and Hannah was standing with the receiver in her hand in the booth beside me. We looked at each other for a moment then back at the phones. We both dialled and waited. We were outside again in less than a minute.

There was no answer, she said.

The line's been cut, I said.

Typical, she said.

At least we tried.

At least we tried, she repeated. It's not like we didn't leave for good reason.

Exactly.

We have to look out for ourselves now.

That's right.

And each other, she said.

I put my arm around her shoulder. Come on. Let's go get some coffee.

We stopped at the first diner we came to, sat down in a booth and waited for the waitress to come over. She was older, maybe forty-something, and had yellow hair that was dark at the roots. She came over to our table and poured coffee into our mugs. She had to lean forward to reach my mug and her large breasts hung down in front of my face. I caught a glimpse of her name stitched onto her uniform and, when she stood up, the writing disappeared around the far side of her chest so that I had to crane my neck in order to read it.

My face is up here, kid, she said. Ready to order?

Sorry, I said. I was just reading the name. I pointed to my own chest.

It's Shelley, sweetheart. Next time just ask. So what'll it be, kids.

Just a coffee for me, I said.

Me too, Hannah said.

Don't you want anything to eat? I asked her.

No, I'm fine, she said.

You sure?

Oh, go on, the waitress said.

Maybe just some toast, she said.

Brown or white?

Brown, please. What about you, John?

I'll have a piece of apple pie, I said and stared after the waitress as she walked off.

What's up? Hannah asked me.

Just thinking, I said and looked out the window at the car park. The windows were streaked and dirty, making it difficult to see outside. Across the parking lot, beyond an island of mowed grass, the traffic on the highway was ongoing. I could just see the tops of cars and trucks passing uniformly like ducks at a shooting gallery. The waitress brought the toast and pie and put the bill down on the table at the same time.

I hate it when they give you the bill right away, Hannah said. Like they want to get rid of you as fast as possible. I think it's rude.

She peeled back the silver tongue on a small plastic container of jam. Her knife blade caught the sun and flicked a bright spot on my chest. The sunlight made the jam look like the squishy inside of an open wound. It glistened and made a faint sucking sound. I poked my fork into the crust of my apple pie. The pastry was perfectly browned and looked fake in the harsh light. I cut off the end with my fork and it tasted like chemicals. Probably came in a cardboard box from a factory.

How's your pie? she asked.

Gross.

I knew these two guys in highschool, she said, spreading jam over a piece of toast, who made a bet about who could be the grossest. They were always doing things to gross each other out. One night one of the guys took this girl out for dinner that they both had crushes on. His friend was at home with a cold, so he figured he was safe. They were having their meal when the other guy walked in. Well, he walked up to the table and horked up this huge wad of phlegm and spat it onto the table. The girl was completely disgusted. I mean, imagine the look on her face? The guy thought he'd won hands down. He said, okay, hand it over, because they'd bet a hundred dollars. But instead of conceding defeat, his friend stood up, bent over and scooped the wad of phlegm up with his tongue and swallowed it. Can you believe it?

No, I said. That's disgusting. How the fuck am I supposed to finish this now? I pushed the pie away.

Sorry, she said.

Did that really happen? I asked her.

That's what I heard.

God, I said.

I lit a cigarette and drank my coffee. I stared out the window and watched a rusty Trans-Am pull up outside the diner.

Wanna go? I asked, after a while.

Ya, I'm ready.

I'll go pay the bill, I said and Hannah got up and headed outside. I went over to the cash and paid the bill and then I went to the bathroom for a piss.

When I walked out to the parking lot, Hannah was giving the finger to these two guys standing by that Trans-Am I'd watched pull in. They were wolf-whistling and the taller of the two was making a humping motion with his hips and arms like he was on some kind of exercise machine. She rolled her eyes and waited for me to get into the car and unlock her door. I felt the need to apologize on their behalf, felt embarrassed and chagrined, but also wondered if I'd ever have the courage to make a pass at her when the time was right.

Do you get that a lot? I asked, once we were back on the highway.

I think every woman does.

Not all of them.

I dunno, I'm not so sure. Guys like that aren't too fussy.

What, fuck anything that moves?

Anything with a hole in it.

Not all men are like that, you know.

Oh, I know that. I'm not talking about all men. Just men like that. But there're enough of them, let me tell you.

You've been with a lot of guys, I said after a while. Haven't you?

I guess, she said softly. What about you?

No, I've never been with a guy.

You know what I mean, she said.

Well, I'm not promiscuous, if that's what you want to know.

You're not a virgin, are you?

No, I said in a voice that was a bit too high-pitched. I've had sex before.

How many times?

I dunno. Why? What about you?

She had to think for a while. I watched her count the fingers on her hands once over, then start again.

Eighteen? she said.

Eighteen? I gasped.

Ya, so? What about you?

Oh, not nearly that many, I said.

How many?

Two or three, I said.

Two or three? she repeated.

I can't remember.

Whaddya mean you can't remember?

I was drunk, I lied.

You're lying.

How come everybody can tell when I'm lying?

So how many? Hannah asked again.

One, I said at last, then swallowed. Just one and just the once.

Hannah nodded her head.

I took another cigarette out of the pack and pushed in the orange knob of the car lighter and waited until I heard it crack back into place. I got into the right lane and overtook a station wagon that was going too slow to be in the fast lane. A little girl with pigtails was sitting in the back seat. She was staring out the window. Our eyes met and she raised a tiny hand and waved at me without smiling.

Do you wanna talk about it? Hannah asked.

No, I said.

That's okay, she said. Maybe you'll tell me one day.

Maybe, I said and looked over at her face and saw for the first time real concern in her dark brown eyes.

Afternoon and the wind was coming through the windows so hot it was like driving straight into a hair dryer. The dashboard was covered in dust and my hair was thick with it. My skin felt itchy. Hannah had taken off her sneakers and was hanging her feet out the window. We stopped at a liquor store and I paid a busker to go in and get us two bottles of JD and a couple of six-packs of Bud. He thanked us and walked off with his guitar slung over his shoulder by a piece of string. We got back into the car and headed east.

Half an hour later, we crossed a river crinkling like tinfoil in the sharp sunlight. I looked down at the water and my whole body yearned for it. I could smell it, the metallic, almost tinny aroma of fresh water.

I wonder if we could go swimming down there? I thought out loud.

Try the next turn-off, Hannah said, and we'll double back.

I veered off the Interstate onto a narrow road and pulled into a gas station just past the exit. An old man with a cowboy hat and boots rose from his chair and sauntered over. He was wearing a bolo tie with a silver Navaho buckle inlaid with a turquoise scarab. His hands were as brown and leathery as old baseball gloves.

Hi there, I said to him

Howdy, he replied. Fill her up? he asked.

Thanks, I said and asked him if there was a swimming hole nearby.

Well, there's the lake, but it's a bit hard to get down to nowadays on account of it all being private property. Though I do know of a café near the water. I think that's your best bet. I know the woman who runs the place. If you ask her nicely, she might just let you go down. Go in for a piece of her sweet potato pie, and I'm sure she will.

How d'ya get there?

Carry on straight till you get to the Baptist church. You can't miss it. Turn right and carry along till you find the Cottonwood Café. Ask for May. You can tell her Harry sent you from the Shell station.

Thanks, I said, paid the old man and drove off.

The café was attached to an old colonial-style house tucked back in an arbor of green trees. It seemed deserted and everything was quiet except for the sound of leaves rustling like dollar bills. We got out of the car and walked into the café, built as an extension onto the side of the house. The interior was cool and dark. The walls were covered in framed pictures of antique cars and cowboys, standing in front of swinging-door saloons. The windows had yellowed blinds drawn down to keep the heat out. After a little while, a very short woman emerged patting a snowy bun into place.

Hello, she said. Just passing through?

We were just wondering if we could take a walk down to

the water and go for a swim? Hannah said.

Harry sent us, I said. From the Shell station.

Figures, she said. He knows I don't like letting strangers use my property. Young people aren't the same nowadays. Why can't you use a pool or somethin' proper?

We've been driving for nearly three days, I said.

She crossed her arms and rested them on her ample breasts.

If I let you go down to the lake, you're not to spend all day down there, you hear? I don't want you wandering willy-nilly all over the place. I don't permit camping, and frankly it makes me uncomfortable to know I've got people hanging about drinking and smoking and misbehaving.

We just want to pop in for a swim, Hannah said. We'll come right back.

I want your wallet as a deposit.

My wallet? I asked.

So as I know you won't go wandering off or stay the night.

How about this? Hannah said and took one of her rings off and gave it to the old woman. We'll be back soon.

The woman considered the ring, took it and cradled it in the palm of her hand. She seemed satisfied with it and didn't bother looking up to watch us leave.

What a cranky old bitch, I said as we walked around to the backyard.

Maybe she has her reasons, Hannah said. She's letting us, after all.

Ya, but it took a bit of convincing. Imagine asking me to leave my wallet?

She's an old woman, John. Maybe she's afraid of a break-in

or somethin'. Maybe she's got somethin' to hide.

She's got enough room to hide it in that big ol' house of hers, I said.

Maybe she's got a mad husband.

I think she's the one that's mad.

Maybe she is, Hannah said. But who cares? Let's go cool off.

I'm into that, I said, feeling a tingling sensation spread out across my chest at the thought of watching Hannah undress. The lawn sloped down and stopped at the edge of some spruce trees. The forest was cool and I could hear the brittle needles crunching underfoot. I could see sunlight flickering off the water down below. I felt the change on my skin as I passed through pools of hot sunshine into cool shade. Voices came skimming across the surface of the water, coming to us as clear and as crisp as if the owners of those voices were standing right beside us. I saw the red hull of a canoe blinking between the tree trunks. We came out onto a flat dirt road that skirted the shore, jumped down out of the woods and walked across a narrow, rocky beach towards the lake. Hannah bent over and took off her shoes. She pulled off her jeans and waded into the water.

You comin' in? she called when she was waist deep.

Ya, ya, I said, in a minute. But first, I wanted to watch her swim. She dove and surfaced, her head slick and shiny as a seal's. She dove again and I watched her kick the air then disappear. She was underwater long enough for the ripples to float out in widening circles like a fading target. She popped up close to the shore and came towards me. I could clearly make out the dark triangle of her pubic hair and two hard nipples under her wet t-shirt.

What? Never seen a woman before?

Fuck off, I said.

Can't you swim? she asked, noticing my reluctance.

Ya, I said. I'm a fish in the water.

You're a chicken is what you are, she said.

And you're a goner, I said, plunging in after her, socks, jeans, t-shirt and all.

I stood ringing out my clothes on the shore, while Hannah lay sunning herself on a rock like a big cat. She sat up and yawned, tapped a cigarette out and stared at the pink sun sinking into a red canyon.

Do you think we should go back? she asked. Make sure May's not loading the shotgun?

Ya, alright, I said. I'm starving.

The forest air was cool through my damp clothes and my muscles felt alert. The thought of Hannah in her wet clothes, rising out of the water like a mermaid, made me hard. I wanted to kiss her, but whenever I felt a twinge of desire it was as if someone was watching me, and my feelings would turn to guilt.

We walked through the trees feeling the sun on our arms like bits of cobweb. When we reached the lawn, Hannah said, I'll race you, and we torpedoed across the grass, onto the gravel drive and around to the side door. I passed Hannah and arrived at the screen door first and pulled it open. I turned and waited for her to come around the corner. I waited a few seconds but still she didn't appear. I walked back around the house and found Hannah sitting on the gravel with one of her jean legs rolled up, brushing the dirt out of a cut on her knee.

What the fuck happened to you?

I fell.

Does it hurt?

Another brilliant question.

Sorry.

Help me up, she said, holding out her hand.

I pulled her up till she was standing, then put my arm around her waist.

I've scraped my knee but I can still walk, she said.

Okay, okay, I said and let her walk ahead of me back into the café. When May saw Hannah's knee, she immediately switched into granny mode.

Are you alright, dear? What happened, for heaven's sake. Oh, I knew those rocks were dangerous.

I just tripped in the parking lot.

Sit down. Sit down. I'll go get some peroxide.

May bustled out through a door and Hannah and I looked at each other and smiled.

Not a bad way to break the ice.

Ya, self-mutilation is always a good way to meet new people, she said.

May came back through the door again and shook her head disapprovingly as she twisted the cap off a bottle of peroxide. She had some cotton balls and a big H-shaped Band-Aid which she put on the table. She soaked the cotton in peroxide, then dabbed Hannah's knee.

There, May said and blew vigorously until it was dry enough for the Band-Aid to stick. She peeled back the white plastic and stretched the H from top to bottom so it covered the scrape. When she was done, Hannah straightened her leg and the Band-Aid buckled. She bent her knee again and I said, Look. H for Hannah.

Are you kids hungry? May asked, sweet as molasses, while Hannah bent to unroll her pant leg. I've got fresh pie and you might as well eat it while it's hot.

I was beginning to think that the only thing people ever ate in America was pie. I sat down across from Hannah, and granny May brought over two large slices of her famous sweet potato pie and two glasses of cold milk. The swimming had worked up our appetites and we ate quickly. I asked the old woman how much we owed but May said it was on the house and not to worry. She wished us a good and safe trip, then walked us to the door and waved good-bye. She shut the door behind us. I heard her lock it, then saw her withered little hand reach up behind the curtain and flip the OPEN sign over to CLOSED. As we were getting into the car, Hannah said, My ring. Just a second.

She walked over to the door and opened the screen and knocked. She waited a while, then knocked again. After a couple of minutes, she knocked harder and for longer until she had to stop and rub her knuckles. I walked over to join her and called out May's name. There was no answer. We walked around to the front of the house and rang the doorbell. I waited a while, then leant on the doorbell for a good minute or so. Hannah walked over to a window and peered inside.

The blinds are down, she said.

We walked all around the house, but every window was blocked by a blind or a curtain. I went to the side door again and shook the handle. Open up! I yelled, but still there was no answer.

Hannah came around the house and said, Never mind. It's not important. It didn't mean that much to me. It's just so weird.

It's spooky, I said. Maybe this is one of those hick towns where everybody's involved in some weird conspiracy. Like in a Stephen King novel.

You're scaring me, John.

We're never going to leave, I teased. Some guy's gonna come out of the bushes, some fucken moron in a lumberjack shirt and size thirteen feet, with a machete and chop us into little bits.

I wanna go, she said. I'm being serious. I don't like this place.

Maybe she's a witch. Right now, May's dropping your ring into some potion and putting a curse on you.

That's not funny, John, she snapped and walked briskly over to the car.

When I inserted the key into the ignition, I turned to her and said, Wouldn't it be typical if the car didn't start and we had to go get help from Harry. Harry at the Shell station.

Can we just get the Mcfuck outta here, please? And I could tell by the look on her face that she really meant it.

Okay, I said. I'm sorry. I'll stop.

I started the car and did a three point turn in the gravel, spun the tires, kicking up a cloud of dust and grit, and took off down the main road back to the highway. It was early evening and purple clouds were forming in the sky to the east, moving swiftly overhead. The sun was setting, casting long shadows across the ground. The light was orange and the trees looked like Halloween pumpkins, glowing bright against a violet sky. I turned to Hannah and said, It's okay now.

I'm glad we're outta there, she said. I'm telling you, what goes around comes around. I took that ring from someone and now someone has taken it away from me.

You stole it?

Ya.

Was it valuable?

Not that much. It was a silver turtle with some turquoise on its back. It was Navaho. When I saw it, I just wanted it. You know what I mean? But from now on, I want a clean slate. If I don't do anything bad, then I'm less likely to have anything bad happen to me.

You think that's how it works?

Well, there's nothing to lose by thinking that way. The worst that can happen is that you have a clear conscience.

I don't think being good has anything to do with it.

Whaddya mean?

If something bad's gonna happen, it just will.

Maybe. But it's like taking an extra precaution, that's all.

Bad things don't just happen to bad people.

I dunno. Call me superstitious, but I don't want to give fate a good reason to come after me.

What about car accidents? I said. You can't protect your-self against them. You could be the best driver in the world.

Okay. But don't you agree the more you know how to drive the more you improve your chances of avoiding an accident?

I guess so. But if something bad happens to me I don't think it's fair to say it's because I've done something bad.

So when are you responsible for what happens to you?

Not all of the time.

And the rest of the time?

I just don't want to be blamed for the things I can't control.

So where do you draw the line? she asked.

Hannah, I said, has anything really, really bad ever happened to you? Something you really, really regret?

Not really. Not that I can think of now.

So maybe you shouldn't talk about things you don't understand.

Gimme a break, she said. That's like saying people who've never been in a war can't talk about it.

Well, maybe they shouldn't.

Ya, right.

I dunno, I said and turned to look at her. I just don't want to be judged, okay?

Ever?

No, I said and switched on the radio because I didn't want to go down that road.

You're gonna have to talk about it someday, John, she said over the music.

About what? I asked.

Whatever it is that's gnawing away at you.

Nothing's gnawing away at me, I said. Besides, I don't have to talk about it if I don't want to.

But you'll never be free of it if you don't talk about it. Ignoring it won't make it go away.

You don't even know what you're talking about!

You're right, but I can sense that something is weighing you down.

Why don't you just shut up, okay?

I was just trying to help.

Well, don't, I said. Not when it comes to this, alright?

The sun went down and neither of us said a word. Hannah seemed upset. I changed course and headed south on the back roads, trying to avoid the fourth of July vacationers with their canoes and surfboards and bicycles, heading for various state recreation areas. The whole blind optimism of it all was getting me down.

Look, I said, finally mustering the courage to broach the subject, I have enough money to pay for a motel room and I could really do with a good night's sleep.

Sure, whatever, she said.

Well, that was easy.

What did you expect?

I dunno. I thought you were still mad at me.

What for?

For telling you to shut up.

Big deal, she said.

I didn't mean it, I said.

Sure you did. But why should I expect any different?

Whaddya mean?

I mean, why should I think you'd want my advice on any-thing? We're just sharing a car to New York and then we'll go our separate ways. I'm not gonna waste my time worrying about your problems. They're *your* fucken problems. What do I care?

I didn't mind, honestly. I was just being defensive. Didn't want to open up old wounds.

You don't have to, she said. I won't ask you again.

[131]

I didn't mean to push you away, I said.

Look, she said, I don't know what your story is. You don't have to tell me if you don't want to.

It's just hard to talk about, that's all. I mean, you're so hard to read. I can't tell what you're thinking.

Next time, don't worry so much about what I'm thinking, she said. I'm not that critical. I'm on your side. That should be a given. Just don't be so harsh with me. I hate being told off.

So we're okay about the motel, then? I asked, turning to her and drinking from the dark pools of her eyes.

Of course we are, she said. You must be exhausted.

I'm shattered, I said.

I kept my eyes peeled for the next sign that said VACANCIES, and at about eleven o'clock in the evening we pulled into the driveway of the Havana Motel, which promised reasonable rates on a flashing billboard by the entrance. I parked outside the main office. Hannah said she'd wait in the car, so I went in alone and a little buzzer rang as I opened the door to the office. There was a counter with a withered geranium and some Budget Rent-a-Car leaflets stacked to one side. The walls were covered in faded wallpaper which was peeling near a leak in the ceiling. Nobody was there but I could see the flickering blue light of a TV through an open door and smelt bacon fat. A game-show host was introducing the next contestant.

A thin young man with a scraggly beard and sweat stains around his armpits came out holding half a club sandwich on a plate. He was still chewing when he greeted me.

Hi there, I said.

[132]

Wanna room? he asked, eyeing me suspiciously.

Ya.

We've only got double rooms left. Same price as a single but you get two double beds which is pretty standard. There's no cable but you can get Pay TV if you want. The price is thirty-five dollars. Check out time is ten o'clock. If you're not out by then, we have to charge you for an extra night. You'll find ice near the pool. The pool closes at ten p.m. and reopens at eight a.m. You swim at your own risk. There's a twenty-dollar deposit when you get your key, which is refunded when you return it. Payment up front, and all telephone calls are charged to your room. Towels are provided, but, uh . . . there's no room service.

I'll be paying cash, I said.

Is that your car? he asked, nodding towards the Omni parked out front.

Yep, I said.

Is that your girlfriend?

I looked over at Hannah. Yes, I said.

Then you'll have to pay for a double room. That'll be fifty-five dollars.

I thought you said the room was thirty-five?

If you're on your own.

But you get two beds, though.

We go by the number of customers, not the room, he said.

Fine, I said and pulled another bill out of my wallet.

I gave a false name and address and paid him the money. He gave me the key and watched me walk out of the office and get into the car. We were in room number 109 which was the first room on the second floor.

We drove around the pool and parked. I picked my jean jacket off the back seat and wrapped it around the two bottles of booze, while Hannah gathered up the cigarettes. We got out of the car, walked up the stairs at one end of the balcony and unlocked the door.

The room smelt of stale cigarette smoke and mildew. There was a low bureau along the left wall, a dirty mirror and a TV. On the right were two double beds with brown covers. The carpet was also brown. The curtains were a faded orange. The bathroom was at the far end of the room. There were two sets of stiff towels and two drinking glasses wrapped in white paper. I brought the glasses back into the room and poured two shots of Jack Daniels. We chinked glasses and Hannah flicked on the TV. She sat on the bed closest to the door while I took the one by the bathroom. We both lit cigarettes and started to smoke. I felt awkward because we'd never been in such a private place. The room was screaming intimacy and I felt like I had to perform or do something, like the situation demanded it. I decided to take a shower.

I'm gonna have a shower.

Ya, sure. I'm gonna watch TV.

Okay, I said and poured some more JD and took the glass into the bathroom. I undressed and kicked everything into a pile in the corner and turned on the water. The pressure was good and I let the water rush over me.

My body went slack and I stood under the shower with my head hung and my arms limp at my sides. I watched the dirt run off my body and a grey swirl disappear down the drain. I washed myself thoroughly, scrubbing behind my ears. I even washed my hair with soap. After a while, I sat down on the floor of the tub and let the water tap me on the head.

I didn't think I was going to be able to make love. The more I wanted to, the more I knew I couldn't, and the more I thought it was the only way to show her how I felt, the more afraid I became. I wanted some sort of commitment, some guarantee she'd stay with me because I knew that, if I had to, I wanted to be the first one to walk away. I didn't want to be the one left hanging. If she didn't feel anything for me then I didn't want to bother. If it wasn't love then I didn't want to risk it, and yet I did. I wanted to know how she felt. The booze and the hot water was making me dizzy. I stood up slowly and held onto the tiled wall of the shower stall until my head stopped reeling. I waited for my stomach to unknot itself. I turned the water off and towelled down. In a minute, I was sweating again. I dried the sweat off my neck and my lower back and behind my knees. I looked at my dirty clothes. I couldn't bare to put them on and decided to wash them later. I wrapped the towel around my waist and opened the door. The air in the room felt cool in comparison and I emerged with the steam billowing out like smoke, like I was walking out of a burning building. Hannah looked up at me.

I went over to my bed and slipped in under the covers. The sheets were threadbare but felt good only because I knew they were clean. The bed was too soft and sagged in the middle. Hannah got up and put out her cigarette in the ashtray and finished the rest of her drink and just missed the corner of the bed as she stumbled over to the bathroom.

Steady, I said.

I'm alright, she said.

She shut the door and I thought of my pile of filthy clothes and wished I had brought them out with me. I lit another cigarette and pulled the covers down to my waist and propped myself up on a pillow and felt the air-conditioning lift the heat off my skin. The sheets were damp beneath me.

I heard the toilet flush and the water running and after a while saw little wisps of steam escaping from under the door. Outside, it was dark and I could hear the faint groan of trucks as they thundered past on the highway. I heard voices and a door slam. A large man in overalls walked past the window. Some music started up on the other side of the wall. I stared at the TV, not watching it, and chain smoked. I glanced towards the bathroom door and got up and brought the bottle of JD over from the bureau and put it on the bedside table. I'd left my glass in the bathroom so I drank straight from the bottle. I got up again and switched off the main light and drew the curtains. I turned on the bedside lamp and got back into bed. I let my eyes go out of focus on the TV screen.

After what seemed like ages, the door opened and Hannah stepped out, naked and pink from the hot water. She walked over and stood at the bottom of the bed.

I sat up.

Can I get in? she asked me.

I couldn't answer her.

Don't you want me to get in? she said.

I still couldn't say anything. My heart was pounding inside my chest and I went clammy all over. I hadn't prepared for this. I was supposed to be the one to make the first move. Not her. Hannah started to fidget in the silence. She brought her hands up and crossed them over her chest. She shifted her weight from one foot to the other.

This is all I have to offer, she said finally. I thought you wanted me, she whispered and her lip quivered.

But do you want me? I asked.

She sat down on the bed. Isn't that obvious?

No, it isn't, I said. It still isn't.

Well, I don't know how you feel either.

I like you, Hannah. I like you a lot. Maybe too much. Oh, for fuck's sake. This is hard for me.

Well, it's hard for me too.

I haven't felt like this about anyone in a long time.

Well, neither have I.

I want you to do this for the right reasons. Not because you feel like you owe me something.

I'll always owe you something. As long as you're paying for everything, I'm powerless.

I'm not asking for anything in return.

But you're not letting me even the score.

This is not some kind of vendetta. I'd want to sleep with you even if you'd been paying your way. What I want to know is would you still want to sleep with me?

I'm not a fucken hooker.

Well then, stop behaving like one.

It's more complicated than that, John.

No, it's not.

Yes, it is. We're not on equal terms. I'm at your mercy.

You could leave.

Exactly. The only way I can affect this relationship is by terminating it. That's the only choice I have.

I don't get it. Are you too proud to accept somebody else's generosity?

Maybe you're the one being proud. You want me to want to sleep with you for all the right reasons. You don't want to acknowledge the other factors at stake, like how indebted I feel.

We're in a fucken motel room on some godforsaken stretch of highway and you're acting like we're negotiating a deal. We're talking about having sex here. Do it if you want to, or don't. And if it's gonna make you feel any better, take what's left of my money. You pay the bills for the rest of the trip.

We sat on the bed quietly for a while, then Hannah started talking in a gentle voice.

When I came out of the bathroom, I just wanted to fool around with you. Maybe have sex. I dunno. When you didn't react, I felt stupid and I got defensive, and wanted to pretend that I wasn't doing it for any emotional reasons. You know, to protect myself.

So you weren't doing it for the money.

Not really.

But a bit.

It's always going to be there. It's not like we love each other.

That's just it. I don't want to put myself on the line for nothing.

Whaddya mean, put yourself on the line? What have you got to lose?

Maybe I really do care about you.

Do you?

Maybe.

Then why don't you just say so, John?

Because I'm scared.

Of what?

It's a risk.

Of course it is. It's supposed to be a risk. It wouldn't be worth anything if it wasn't.

I don't want to lose again.

It's not a contest.

You don't understand.

Then tell me.

Never mind.

What do you want?

Nothing, I said and turned away. I snuggled down into the bed and pulled the covers up and pretended to sleep. Hannah got up and walked over to her bed and got in between the sheets. I reached over and switched out the light.

I lay for a long time with my arms under my head staring at the ceiling. Finally, I got out of bed and walked over and sat down beside her. I brushed the hair off her face. Her eyes were shut like tiny fists. I whispered, Hannah, are you awake?

What do you want? she mumbled without opening her eyes.

I'm sorry, I said.

Hannah shifted. She turned over onto her back and pulled her hand out from under the covers and put it on my leg. I'm not your enemy, John. I'm right here, and for now, I'm not going anywhere.

But later . . .

Don't think about that. You should learn to trust people.

Hannah, I asked, have you ever been in love?

No, she said.

I bent down and kissed her forehead. So you're still a virgin, then.

That's not how I feel, but I guess you could put it that way, she said and put her hand behind my head and pulled my mouth towards hers.

When I woke up, we were spooning. It was hot under the covers and I had to peel my skin away from hers. I got up and felt the muscles around my skull contract like snapped elastics. I walked over to the bathroom and splashed cold water on my face. It was Sunday, July 3rd, and the third morning I'd spent with Hannah. I looked down at my penis and it was covered in dried cum which flaked off under my fingernail. I brought my hand to my nose and smelt a mixture of metal and salt. When I got out of the shower, I looked down at our dirty clothes on the floor and decided to wash them in the bathtub with hand soap. Hannah appeared in the doorway wrapped in a blanket while I was bent over scrubbing my jeans.

I feel like shit, she said.

Me too.

Don't worry about mine, she said, looking at the soapy clothes in the bath.

It's okay. They're almost done, I said.

Thanks.

By the time I was dressed, I was shivering from the dampness of my clothes. I opened the door and stepped out onto the balcony. The warm air was a relief after the air-conditioning and I leaned up against the rail and smoked a cigarette and watched some kids playing in the pool. I went back inside and turned on the TV to find out what time it was. It was nine-fifty. I told Hannah that we had ten minutes to check-out time and she came hopping out of the bathroom, tying up the laces on one of her sneakers.

We'd better go, she said.

I'll meet you at the car. I'm going down to the office.

We hit the desert by mid-day under a broiling sun and turned onto a back road and headed north. The earth was brick-red. The sky a scintillating blue. The ground was dotted with granite-coloured bushes, low-lying and speckled with yellow flowers. The wind rushed in at the window. The sun bit into our flesh. This country was harsh and unforgiving. There was no room for error or miscalculation.

Hannah and I drank warm beer and ate the beef jerky we'd bought that morning. She was holding her hair up with her hands, trying to dry the sweat off the back of her neck. Her hair had auburn streaks in the light and her arms looked like they'd been dipped in honey. We didn't talk about the night before. I figured we didn't have to. I figured she was mine.

She sighed and said, Better be careful with our cigarette butts. I wouldn't want to start a brush fire.

The mountains looked like coals. The ground was shimmering from all the heat rising off the earth.

I used to think, Hannah said, that the worst thing in the world was winter. Now I'm not so sure. At least you can dress up against the cold, protect yourself. This heat, though, you can't escape it. Your skin would eventually buckle and peel off like paint. Just think of how many miles in either direction this goes on for. Just sand and cactus trees. Looks like the bottom of the ocean, all the plants look like seaweed. We could be driving across the ocean floor right now in a submarine with hundreds of feet of water over our heads.

Maybe it was an ocean once, I said.

It's so desolate. You'd die out here before anyone found you. I'd hate to run out of gas.

Me too, I said and checked the fuel gauge.

This must be what hell is like. All the space and time and freedom in the world but you just can't escape the heat. Wherever you go . . .

Hannah pulled her body out the window and sat on the sill, so all I could see were her legs. She started tapping a rhythm on the roof of the car, then quickly slid back in.

The roof's too hot to hold on to. It's like a grill up there. Too bad we don't have a couple of burgers, eh John? she said in a southern drawl. We could have a Bar-B-Que.

I relish the idea, I said and smiled to myself.

I looked at the fuel gauge again. The indicator was nearly touching the red. We would have to refuel soon, and I was beginning to worry when I saw what looked like a gas station down the road in the distance.

As we drew nearer, it became clear that it had been abandoned years ago. I slowed the car down to get a good look as we drove past. There was a low building with shattered windows and two stumps of pipes and wires, like decapitated robots, where the old gas pumps must have been. I could just make out a trace of the golden shell on a faded billboard. It was like coming across a carcass of bleached bones. I half expected to see the shadow of a vulture's wings travel across the road, but there was nothing above except the endless, cobalt sky.

I heard a story once, Hannah said without looking at me, about a family that set off across the Sahara. They got lost in a sandstorm and wandered for days after they ran out of gas. They started to die of thirst. They drank their own urine until they couldn't pee anymore. Then in a act of desperation, they sacrificed one of their own children so they could eat it. The horrific thing is that they survived. They were rescued shortly after that.

God, I said.

Could you do that? Eat your own child?

I dunno.

I couldn't. No way.

I don't think we know until it happens. I kind of think I might. I mean, if I thought I was gonna die if I didn't.

But at any cost? she asked.

I don't think you really stop to think about it. You just try to survive. In the end, we're just animals. That's all we are, you know.

No, we're not. We're humans, that's the whole goddamn point. We can choose not to do something that's beneath us, as a matter of principal.

Ya, but I ain't no martyr.

Obviously not.

And I'm not gonna risk my neck to be some kind of fucken hero.

You never know, she answered. They say heroes are ordinary people reacting in a situation. They don't have time to think . . .

Like those people in the desert?

That's completely different. Saving someone from drowning, say, is completely different from eating one of your own children.

What do you know about drowning? Have you ever seen anybody drown? You make it sound like any old Joe-blow could just reach out and save them.

I never said it was easy. It's not. That's what makes it heroic.

Oh, and you know about these things, do you?

No, she said sadly. I've never done anything heroic in my life . . .

We'd long passed the deserted gas station but I continued to drive slowly down the road as if the weight of memory was tangible and heavy, as if I was hauling a huge trailer behind me. The further back I remembered, the harder it was to move forward.

I'm way too selfish, Hannah said at length.

Guess that makes two of us.

When the going gets tough, she said, I get going. I hate it sometimes.

I looked over at Hannah. A little bead of sweat departed from the hair above her temple and slid down the side of her face, disappearing under the curve of her chin. I turned back to the rippling road and sped up again. Everything was melting like wax. I could imagine the tires sticking to the asphalt, leaving two black trails like streaks of mascara across the desert. I checked the fuel gauge again. We needed gas.

We drove on for another five miles or so until a sign appeared like a lollipop down the road. I slowed down as it approached. It read, LAST CHANCE TEXACO, 9 MILES.

Hannah looked at me and said, Last chance, John. She

reached over and squeezed my thigh. I looked back at her and tried to smile.

Nine miles later, I veered off into the Texaco station. Just the rattle of loose gravel underneath, following the car's dark shadow like a shark slicing its way through the light. The gas station looked like it had been dropped from the sky, as if it had once been part of a movie set, but the movie had long been made and all the crew gone home. There was nothing around for miles. We drove over a cable and a little bell chimed. I parked the car beside a pump and we both got out. I walked over to the front of the car and touched the hood. It was burning hot. The engine was creaking and popping with heat.

We might have to let the car cool down a bit. I don't want to overheat it, I said.

Man, Hannah said, stretching her back, this is wild.

I walked over to the building that served as an office and garage. I pulled the screen door forward on its spring hinge. There was nobody behind the counter, or in the bathroom, or in the small garage where a couple of greasy tools, second-hand tires and oil cans lay scattered on the floor. I walked back outside and looked around for Hannah. I found her around the side of the building staring at a man asleep under a cowboy hat, propped up in the shade of a shiny red Coke machine. He had his arms crossed and was wearing a brand-new, dark blue pair of jeans over a dusty pair of cowboy boots. Hannah just stood there, watching the man beside the Coke machine with the wide empty desert as a backdrop. It was strange. I felt like we had intruded, had trespassed into

[145]

his livingroom, found him asleep and were about to have the audacity to wake him up.

Guess this is the guy who runs the place, she said to me. I hate to wake him up.

We could hang out for a while, I said.

Ya, she said and stared off into the distance. You know what I really want? she asked me.

What?

A Coke.

Go for it, I said and handed her a couple of quarters.

Just to commemorate the moment.

Ya, I know what you mean, I said. I'll leave you to it.

I walked back over to the car and put my hand on the hood, then walked out onto the road and stood right in the middle on the faded yellow line. I stared as far as I could in one direction, and then I turned and stared as far as I could the other way. There was nothing except a shimmering grey ribbon of tarmac like a vein cutting through miles of dry red earth. I listened to the breeze in my ears. I stood there for a couple of minutes until the top of my head started to burn in the sun. I wiped my brow with the back of my wrist and headed back around the building to where Hannah was standing. She was still staring at the man with the cowboy hat.

I think he's dead, she said.

He's not dead. He's sleeping.

No, I think he's dead, she said again.

How do you know? I asked her.

Because he hasn't moved.

That's because he's sleeping. Here, I said and took the

quarters from her hand and inserted them into the machine and pushed the big rounded Coke button and a can came shooting down like a tobogganist. When the can came clanging down, the man bucked like a spooked horse. He kicked the air and bolted upright, dropped his Stetson and scrambled to his feet.

Howdie, he said, smacking the dust off his jeans and picking up his hat. Y'all want some gas?

Yep, I said, that's the general idea, and we followed the cowboy round the building and over to the car. He adjusted his hat and took a pouch of tobacco out of his pocket and rolled a cigarette. He lit up and stood there smoking and spitting little bits of tobacco off his tongue onto the ground, rocking on the heels of his cowboy boots. I looked at Hannah and she shrugged, downed the last of her Coke, then wiped her mouth with the back of her hand and dropped the can into a bucket near her feet.

Do you mind if I fill her up? I asked, nodding towards the pumps.

Not at all, the cowboy said, turning his cigarette around and staring at the burning end.

I put twenty-three dollars in the tank and took some money out to pay the man. He reached into the pocket of his jean jacket for some change and withdrew a two-dollar bill.

Y'all have a safe trip now, y'hear.

Thanks, I said and watched him saunter back to his shed and get in behind the counter and sit down.

What a guy, Hannah said.

Ya, I said, the real McCoy.

I showed Hannah the two-dollar bill. They don't make

these anymore, I said. It'll be worth a lot of money in a few years from now.

Ya, like in fifty.

Still, they're rare. Here, you have it.

No, no. You keep it, John.

No, I'm serious. I want you to have it. As a memento. I want you to keep it.

Really?

Ya, you can give me a blow-job later on, I said and poked her in the ribs.

Aw, fuck you, she said and punched me in the arm, then ran round to the other side of the car.

I mean it, I said and handed her the bill across the top of the car.

So do I, she said and took it from me. She smoothed it flat on the roof, folded it in half, scraped the folded edge with her fingernail, then ripped it in two. She handed me a piece, folded the other half and put it in the front pocket of her jeans.

We pulled out of the gas station and continued down the road. There was no one else around and I felt unleashed. Just the wide open desert stretching before us and the hot sun winking off the hood of the car. I watched the Texaco sign recede in the rearview mirror. Hannah turned the radio on and we bopped along in time to the music. She was waving her arms around and mouthing the words. I felt happier than I had in a long time.

I'm having a really good time, Hannah said, as if she'd read my mind.

Ya, me too, I said. D'ya wanna drive?

What, me? she said. Finally.

I pulled over and left the car running and we both got out and changed places. Hannah gave me a wink, stepped on the clutch and put the car in gear. She accelerated past second into third and cruised into fourth.

Very smooth, I said.

Well, I can drive, she said. I just don't have a license.

It was nice to be in the passenger seat. I fiddled with the radio. I put my arm on the window sill and leant my head out so my face was in the wind. I took great bites of air. My cheeks ballooned out and my gums dried up. When I closed my mouth, everything stuck. My eyes started to water and the tears trickled across my temples and into my hair. I rested my chin in the crook of my elbow and felt the warmth of the afternoon sun on my skin. I saw a bird circling in the sky and thought of the seagulls back home. I watched it ascend in spirals, leisurely floating on a rising air current up into the azure sky. Red earth. Blue sky. Not a drop of water for miles. For the first time in ages, I missed the ocean.

I watched Hannah stare out at the road. She seemed deep in thought or maybe she was just concentrating on the driving. Either way, I left her alone and watched the telephone poles flash by like railroad tracks. My eyes fixed on the wire strung up between the poles like the line on a cardiograph, rising and falling with every heart beat. Red earth. Blue sky.

I hadn't really seen the desert the way I was looking at it now. It was like the flat cracked palm of an old man.

Towards evening, we stopped at a little roadside café. It was

called the Desert Flower and was painted pink and white.
There was a trailer to one side with a line of washing out back
and a dog on a chain that started barking as we pulled up.
We got out and stretched our legs. The air was still. No wind.
It was holding all the heat of the day. My legs felt sweaty in
my jeans and I wondered how much I'd regret it if I cut them
into shorts. I pulled at my t-shirt where it was plastered to
my back. Hannah got out of the car and shook her legs.

My leg's stiff from holding the gas pedal down, she said.
What this car needs is automatic pilot. Some cars have that,
you know. You can program them to drive along at a constant speed.

Ya, I know, I said and headed into the café. What d'ya
wanna eat?

What are you gonna have? she asked.

Hamburger and fries.

How's your money, John? she asked.

It's okay. We'll get to New York alright.

And then what?

I haven't really thought that far, I said.

I mean, what are you gonna do once you get there?

I dunno.

Do you know anybody there?

No.

So why are you going?

Like I said, I wanted to get out of California.

But why New York?

I've never been.

Aren't you afraid?

Of what?

[150]

I dunno. Getting mugged. Not having any money, anywhere to stay.

I've kinda gotten used to that. I seem to get by alright.

Ya, she said and stared at the menu printed out on a paper place-mat. You know, John, you could come up to Montreal with me. We could get an apartment. You could work under the table. You're Canadian. You could get a social insurance number . . .

You make it sound so easy.

Well, how complicated would it be?

Aw, come on. You'd get back. You'd meet up with old friends. Your family would want you back.

I dunno, John.

You wouldn't want me there after a while.

Yes, I would.

Really?

Absolutely.

I dunno, I said. It'd be a big risk.

Hannah sighed.

It would really depend on you, I said.

That's right, I forgot. The risk factor. I'm just not reliable enough. Can't be sure I'm gonna stick around forever, she said and looked away.

I dropped my head into my hands and rubbed my forehead. A young girl came over to our table and asked us what we wanted to eat. She was wearing a large pair of glasses with pink plastic frames that came halfway down her cheeks. The lenses were thick, Coke bottle glasses, and they made her eyes look huge and out of proportion. She was shy and nervous and spent a long time writing down exactly what I ordered. Not *ham, AD*, but *hamburger, all-dressed*, as if she were afraid of forgetting what she'd written by the time she got back to the kitchen. Hannah spoke quietly when it was her turn to order. She lit a cigarette and said, Never mind. Do what you want, John. I don't care.

I felt like I was swimming through a lake and I'd just hit a cold patch. If I went with you, I said, I'd have to be absolutely sure you weren't gonna change your mind one day.

Why? I don't understand. People change. You're gonna change. You wouldn't want me to make you promise never to change your mind about something for the rest of your life.

I'm not talking in general. What I'm trying to say is that when you feel really strongly about someone that feeling never goes away.

Aw, come on.

I know how I feel.

Feelings fade, John.

Not in my experience, Hannah. It's all or nothing with me.

Always on your terms, eh, John?

I don't want to lose you.

But what you don't seem to understand is that you don't even have me to begin with. You're so afraid of losing me that you haven't even bothered trying to win me over in the first place. It's like you've skipped the dating stage altogether and gone straight for the commitment. I mean, you're already anticipating the break-up. Ever hear of a self-fulfilling prophecy? You worry so much about the bad things that might occur, you don't leave room for anything good to hap-pen, or anything to happen at all. Anyways, who's to say you wouldn't be the one to leave me. You're the one who's so preoccupied with it. Maybe I should be asking myself the same questions about you.

I looked around the café. There was a lone trucker at the counter but, apart from that, we were the only other customers in the joint. I could hear a clock ticking behind my head and turned around. It was seven-thirty in the evening. I wanted to hold onto that moment. I wanted to trap it, to stop time, because I didn't know what was going to happen. I didn't want to know. I couldn't control the outcome but I wanted Hannah to know how desperately I needed this to work. It's been a good day, was all I could think of to say.

Hannah looked at me and laughed. Yeah, it has, she said. I guess we'll just have to leave it at that for now. Best that we can hope for, eh?

The waitress came over and placed two glasses on the table. I sat there drinking my Coke through a straw and listening to the sound of that clock like it was trying to tell me something. The trucker stood up, threw some change on the counter and left the café.

When we had finished and the girl had brought the bill and put it down on the table, Hannah said, Let's dine and dash.

What? I asked.

Ya, she said. Nobody's around. They won't catch us.

I dunno, I said.

Look, you're running out of money, right?

But the bill's not even ten bucks.

Still. It's ten more bucks in your pocket.

I suppose.

I'll pretend I'm going to the bathroom. There was a sign for one outside around the back. I'll start the car and you can come running out.

I guess so, I said, and Hannah got up and told me in a loud voice that she was going to take a leak and glanced back as she was walking out the door.

I sat with my hands in my lap. I watched the girl behind the counter spoon out a little portion of rice pudding into a bowl and sit down on a stool to eat it. I could hear the clang of dishes in the kitchen. I imagined the girl's father working up a sweat over the grill. When she'd go in to tell him we'd made a run for it, he'd hit her across the face with the back of his hand. Her glasses would go flying.

I put ten bucks on the table which meant she'd get a two-dollar tip and then I left the café. When I got through the door, I started running. I ran up to the car and jumped in. I yelled at Hannah to Go! Go! Go!

She sped out of the parking lot and back onto the highway. My heart was pounding fast and I could feel the sting of tears in my eyes. I felt ashamed and my heart still burned with the image of that little girl, miles away from any friends, serving truckers at a truck-stop café all day, pouring coffee and making change.

Hannah let out a yelp. Excellent! she screamed. See? I knew we could do it.

She was driving fast but I didn't care. I just wanted to get drunk. We still had a bottle of JD and a few cans of beer left. I climbed over the seat and sat down in the back and picked the bottle up off the floor. I opened it and took a large mouthful. It burned its way down my throat and sent a spasm through my body, then a pacifying heat spread out from my stomach. The windows were open and Hannah's hair was flying around her head like bats in a cave. I sat in the middle of the seat with my palms on the upholstery, watching the road ahead.

What are you doing back there? she asked.

Drinking, I said.

Can I have some? she asked.

Ya, I said and climbed back in front and passed her the bottle. She handed it back to me and said, Thanks. Let's just enjoy ourselves, okay?

That's the plan, Stan, I said and lit another cigarette.

Hannah drove while I got drunk. She'd take occasional sips but by the time the sun went down I was hammered and she was still driving in a straight line. We were heading north and Hannah's face was dark against the sky behind her, which was as red as the torn flesh inside a blood orange. The sun was almost down and the sky to my right was indigo and black. The first few stars of the evening were out and I tried to make a wish but couldn't concentrate. The air was cool. It was a welcome relief. The night closed in on us until, eventually, I couldn't see past the headlights. The car felt cozy and self-contained, like a submarine or a spaceship. The radio murmured softly. I punched the cigarette lighter and waited for it to pop out. I pulled it out and it went flying into my lap. By the time I got hold of it, I had burned a hole in the seat.

What the fuck is going on? Hannah asked. What the fuck is that smell?

Burnt the upholstery, I slurred.

The what?

Up-holster-y, I pronounced deliberately.

Oh, she said.

Wannothersip? I asked, waving the bottle in front of her face.

Yes, please. You've been hogging it all night.

This time she took a really long swig. I watched her throat rise and fall with each swallow. I loved that neck. I wanted to kiss it. I wanted it to be mine. I didn't want it any other way.

I'm in love with you, I said and fell onto her shoulder.

You're drunk is what you are, she said, although I felt her hand come up and smooth the hair across my temple just before I slipped from consciousness into oblivion like a sinking ship that waits, then plunges into the water, dragging whatever is on the surface down with it.

I woke shivering in the dawn. The windows were covered in condensation. My muscles were cramped and aching. I wiped the window and saw in the distance the black pointy tops of coniferous trees standing out against a pale green sky. The interior of the car was a metallic grey in the early morning light. I looked down at my pink hands and studied the dirt under my nails and my ragged cuticles. My mouth tasted like iron. I sat up, still drunk from the night before. It was Monday morning, the fourth of July, and the first morning since Friday that I hadn't woken up beside Hannah. I could barely focus. I opened the door and slid my legs out. I was surrounded by wheat fields. In contrast to the desert, the land was ripe and active. The wheat was hushed and trembled. The air was cool and full of the sound of birds chirping.

The car was parked at a deserted rest stop. There was a gravel shoulder two car-widths wide, in the shape of a semi-circle, with a grassy border running the whole length with a couple of picnic tables scattered here and there. I rose unsteadily to my feet and looked over the car down the rest stop at a red pick-up truck. The cab was empty and there was no one in sight. I couldn't see Hannah and my first thought was that she'd left me. I'd told her I loved her and she had decided to leave. Maybe I deserved it. Maybe I was fated to lose everyone I ever cared about, but that didn't make it any easier this time round. I felt betrayed. How could I have been so stupid to trust a girl like that?

I lit a cigarette, took a drag and my stomach rolled over. I felt nauseous. I walked across the gravel and onto the grass. I stood there for a while and finished the whole cigarette despite how sick it was making me feel. I tried to be rational. Maybe she'd gone off to pee somewhere. Maybe she was getting coffee. Maybe she'd found a soft place in the grass to fall asleep, and then I heard a voice coming from the direction of the pick-up truck. I heard a woman laugh and I knew that it was Hannah.

I tried to walk quickly but I was too drunk. I staggered towards the other end of the lot and got a flash of my dad arriving home late one night after a particularly bad binge, propelling himself like a bumper car through the livingroom until he reached the sofa. I felt the sting of his back hand on my face and felt the old humiliation rise in me like bile. I could taste it.

I got up to the truck and put a hand out to steady myself. I could now see behind it to where the grass ended and the farm fields began. Hannah was there, sitting on a picnic table beside a man with long, blue-black hair. They were facing the other way and talking, looking out across the fields and watching the clouds turn pink as the sun began to rise. The man said something and Hannah laughed, leaning into him a bit. It was like they were sharing a private joke. Their bodies were relaxed and intimate. Anger reared inside me like a caged animal refusing to be contained. I commanded my legs forward and lurched on the gravel. They both swung around as if they'd been caught. Hannah got up and so did the man. He was tall, slightly older, and had a strong body. He came towards me with a smile on his face.

I can see what you mean, he said. Must have Indian blood. Can't handle the booze. You're still drunk, my friend, he said and put his hand on my shoulder.

Get off of me, I growled.

Relax, he said, withdrawing.

Don't tell me to relax, I said. Hannah, where the fuck have you been?

Hannah's shoulders dropped a couple of inches. You were dead to the world, she said, coming over. I just thought I'd stretch my legs. I've been talking to Jimmy, here.

Thought it'd be a good time to make your escape?

What are you talking about? Hannah said.

We were just having a conversation, Jimmy said.

Shut up, I said.

Who you telling to shut up?

Please, Hannah said. Let's not fight about this.

This is none of your fucken business, I said to Jimmy.

Well, I might just stick around and make it my business, he said.

What do you care? I asked him.

I don't, he said. Not about you, at any rate.

But I bet you've got your eye on Hannah, here.

Just for the moment, maybe.

John, Hannah said. Let's just talk this over.

I don't think he's in the mood to talk, Jimmy said.

Please, she repeated.

You know, I think he's jealous.

You're not helping, Hannah said. Please don't make this any worse.

Ya, you fucken asshole, I said.

John! Hannah snapped. What the hell's the matter with you?

As if you don't know.

That's right, I don't.

Well, I shouldn't have to spell it out for you.

Hannah took a step closer and softly said, Please, John, tell me what this is all about. I wanna know.

I looked over at Jimmy who was standing with his legs apart and his arms crossed over his chest. I turned to Hannah and lowered my voice. I finally get the courage to tell you I love you, and what do you do? You fucken hightail it the first chance you get.

I haven't gone anywhere, Hannah said. Besides, it wasn't courage, it was the alcohol talking.

Ya, you're brave now, but you won't be when that wears off, Jimmy said.

Would you please stop provoking him, Hannah said.

Don't worry, I said to her, I couldn't give a fuck about him. He's just a goddamn Indian.

I'm a what? Jimmy said, moving forward. You don't know shit, man.

Please! Hannah shouted, raising her arms and standing between us.

What did you tell him? I asked her.

Whaddya mean, what did I tell him?

What's going on between you two?

Nothing!

Then why's he so protective of you?

I dunno.

You did, I said.

Did what?

You probably fucked him already.

Grow up, John, she said.

Hey buddy, I said to Jimmy. Did you give her some money for it? That really turns her on. She likes getting paid for it.

Fuck you! Hannah screamed.

I think you'd better just shut your mouth, Jimmy said.

How 'bout I make you shut yours!

I'd like to see you try, he said.

Stop it! Hannah yelled, pushing me backwards. Just stop it! You've got it all wrong, John.

Bullshit!

It's true!

You're a fucken slut, Hannah.

Fuck you, she said. You don't trust anybody, do you? How do you ever expect to have a relationship with anybody?

You want out of this relationship? I screamed. You got it. You're out.

I was never in it, she said. You wouldn't let me. I'm the one who asked you to come to Montreal with me, remember? But what did you say? You'd be taking a big risk, wasn't that it?

Too big, eh? Well, *you're* the fucken liability, John. I don't need to take this shit from you.

Hannah's face was red and blotchy. I could see a vein throbbing at her temple. I wanted to say I was sorry. I wanted to hold her and tell her I'd never leave her but I couldn't find the words. My mouth felt like it was full of sand and there was no room for my tongue to move.

Hannah turned to Jimmy and said, Can we get out of here? Right now? I mean, I don't know this guy. I just met him. Please?

Jimmy looked at me standing dead in my tracks. All of a sudden, he seemed sorry for me. He looked back at Hannah and shrugged his shoulders and said, Ya, I guess so.

Let's go, she said and I watched her walk over and get into his truck. She sat very still in the passenger seat with her head bent. She wouldn't look at me. Jimmy started the truck and backed out of the parking lot. He turned the truck around and pulled out onto the highway. She never looked back. Not once.

I sat in the car for a while and tried to collect myself. I couldn't believe what had happened. I couldn't understand where my anger had come from. The more I thought about it the more I realized what a terrible mistake I'd made. I could have gone with Hannah all the way to Montreal. I'd had the chance to be with someone and I'd blown it.

I started the car and drove off in the direction they had gone. I saw a hitchhiker on the road but it wasn't her. I checked every car I passed to see if Hannah was in it. At one point, I thought I saw her in the cab of a sixteen-wheeler as it was signalling to exit and followed it into a gas station. I walked over to the truck but it was somebody else.

I carried on in this zigzag way for two more days, gliding slowly past motels, checking every rest-stop café. I even asked a waitress if she had seen a girl travelling on her own or maybe with another person, but I had no luck. Hannah was gone, vanished, lost accidentally like a ring you were wearing when you went into the sea and which takes you hours to realize is missing from your finger because the feel of it has lingered long after the ring slipped off.

Part Three

I drove through Oklahoma and Missouri, through the southern tip of Illinois, into Indiana and Ohio. I crossed the border into Pennsylvania on July 16th, 1988, at 10.37 a.m. I can remember the exact date and time of day because I passed a billboard for Rolex watches by the side of the road. At first I'd thought it was an ad for some religious group because it said, in bold block letters on a plain white background, THE TIME HAS COME, but then as I got closer I saw the Rolex name in the bottom right-hand corner. Across the top of the ad was a digital clock with the date, alternately flashing with the time of day. I liked the precision of the numbers. They seemed to remind me that I was still in the world, that I hadn't got entirely lost. It was something concrete I could hold on to, something I could be really sure of because, after Hannah left, there wasn't much I felt that I could count on.

Just outside of Pittsburgh, I stopped at a café and had coffee and toast. I sat by the window and watched a woman across the street weed her garden. She spent a whole hour on her knees, pulling plants out of the ground and putting them into a black garbage bag. When that was full, she carried it over to the driveway and went into the house for another one. She stretched her back, looked up at the clouds brewing overhead, then crouched down again, clearing the ground underneath a spruce hedge. She stood up and walked across the lawn over to a rose bush that was growing by a brook that ran underneath the road. She started to prune it, dropping whole branches to the ground. At one point, she carried a small bouquet of yellow roses back into the house. After a while, I got up and went outside. I looked up at the sky, down at the key in my hand then back at her house. I started the car and drove off.

I got it into my head that I was destined to be the interminable tourist, that I would always feel like a foreigner everywhere I went, that somehow I would never put down roots, never have a home or a family. I pitied myself instantly and this pity gave me comfort. A picture started to gel in my mind, something along the lines of the wandering cowboy, the Marlboro man, and I drew another cigarette out of my pack and lit up. I tilted my head to one side and blew smoke out of my nostrils, then all of a sudden it started to rain. The sky cracked open with a thunderous clap and the rain came pouring down. It was the first rain I'd seen in weeks and it seemed to confirm my mood just then and I felt like it was raining for my benefit, a kind of hats-off from nature. I could hear it pelting down on the roof of the car and the sound was loud and hollow. I switched the wipers on and they pulsed across the windshield to a steady, dull beat. The rain, gathered to the tips of the wipers, streamed sideways off the car. It was warm summer rain and I left my window open. My arm got soaked and the side of my face. The end of my cigarette sizzled and went out.

By late afternoon, I had turned north and was heading towards the Catskill mountains in New York State. The countryside was hilly and lush and I drank in all the various

[166]

shades of green, almost blue through that veil of rain. I looked over at my wallet on the passenger seat. I was running out of money. I'd been driving for two weeks, meandering north-eastward, taking all the back roads, making the journey to New York City last as long as possible. I felt sober, not only because I hadn't had a drink since Hannah left, but because everything seemed to have come into sharp focus.

I liked the slick black surface of the road, the way it deepened into a canal, the way the spray came shooting off the car in front as if it were a speedboat. When night fell, the air grew cool and I turned the heat on. My life had shrunk and seemed to be contained within the four walls of my car, did not extend past the fogged-up glass of the windows and it was all that I could handle. I felt safe and protected in my hard shell. I reached over and turned the radio on. I was driving along a dark, deserted stretch of road when all the power in my engine cut out and I started to coast. I flicked my hazards on and rolled over to the side and braked. I heard a low rumble and a truck lumbered past burying me in its wet wake. My car shuddered from the pressure of the wind that followed it. The engine was turning over but the car wouldn't move. I revved it for a while until my headlights started to grow dim. I leaned forward and dropped my forehead down onto the steering wheel. The rain, like impatient fingers, carried on drumming the roof.

After a while, I decided to leave my car and go for help. I hadn't passed anything for miles so figured the best thing to do was walk ahead. I put my wallet in my back pocket, opened the door and stepped outside. I locked the car and pulled my jean jacket tight around my neck. I started down the road at a quick pace, feeling the rain soak through to my shoulders. Soon my jeans were heavy and sticking to my thighs. My feet started to squelch inside my sneakers. A car passed in the opposite direction and I raised both arms and waved. It didn't even slow down and I had to jump back to avoid the spray. There were trees to either side and I could hear the rain dripping through the leaves. It was pitch-black and I started to feel uneasy. I turned around and saw the outline of my car in the headlights of another one approaching in the distance. I stood and waited. When it got closer, I started to wave frantically. The car slowed down and I could see the driver peer over at me. It was a woman and I started to explain that my car had broken down. I pointed down the road and she shook her head, raising her hands helplessly, then drove on again. I watched the reflection of her red brake lights skim the road, then disappear around a bend.

I walked for what seemed like hours. Cars were rare and nobody felt inclined to stop. I gave up trying to wave them down and stuck to the gravel shoulder occasionally stumbling ankle-deep into potholes full of water. The rain didn't let up and I started to shiver. I clenched my fists and blew into them. I wiped my nose with the back of my hand. At one point, I noticed a metal barrier along the road to my right, luminous in the first grey shades of dawn. I went over and looked down. At the bottom of a steep gully, I could see the black vein of a river. I could just make out the lighter flecks where the surface was broken by rocks or rapids. I could barely hear the water above the noise of the rain dripping through the undergrowth. I followed the ravine with my eyes and saw a bridge in the distance.

The sky to the east was clearing and a pale yellow light creeping over a ridge of trees. The rain was gentler then, and the clouds overhead had a mauve tint to them. The road began to slope down towards the river. I crossed an old covered bridge and walked past a sign that said, WELCOME TO BRIDGEWATER, ESTIMATED POPULATION 315. There was a square red-brick building to the right that might have been a schoolhouse once, and on the far side of the road, on the bank of the river, stood a row of simple wooden houses in various states of disrepair. All the windows were dark, so I continued down the street listening to the crunch of my soles on the gritty pavement. I passed a big house on my right, eerily quiet, with a wraparound porch. It was blue with white shutters, and had a flag pole on the front lawn with the star-spangled banner hanging limp and dripping twenty feet in the air.

Past the house on my right was a gravel driveway that opened out into a parking lot in front of a store that was locked up for the night. The store was on the first floor of a large farmhouse. The front door was painted red and there was a CLOSED sign hanging in the window. There was an oval sign at the edge of the parking lot that said, THE APPLESEED EMPORIUM, HEALTH FOOD STORE. I was about to walk away when a light came on inside. I went up to the door, climbed the three steps and, pressing my face against the glass, peered inside.

Behind the checkout counter was a stairway leading up to the second floor. I saw a man come down the stairs carrying a crate of empty milk bottles. He walked to the opposite end of the store and disappeared through a doorway. I heard a screen door squeak open then clap shut, and stepped down off the stoop. Parked at the end of the driveway round the side of the house was a red Dodge van with the back doors propped wide open. I heard the door again and continued round the back. A few rickety steps led up to an enclosed porch built onto the rear of the house. There was a large back-yard sloping down to a row of brambles and a neat rectangular vegetable patch running the length of the lawn on the far side, each green row marked off by a seed packet perched on top of a popsicle stick. The grass was silver and rainwater was rushing out of the gutter into a puddle by the steps.

The door opened again and the man came out carrying two more empty plastic milk crates. He carried them over to the van and set them down inside. He turned around and caught sight of me standing in the driveway, hair plastered to my head and dripping from top to toe. We looked at each other for a moment. He was tall and older, in his thirties, and was wearing jeans and an orange sweatshirt from Cornell University. He had a full head of curly brown hair, a thick brown beard, and was wearing a pair of round, gold-rimmed glasses flecked with raindrops and slightly misted over. He looked surprised, but came forward after a while and said, Hi there.

Hi, I answered back and extended a cold red hand. My car broke down.

Bad night for it, he said.

It's a little wet, I said and sniffled.

How far away is it?

I dunno, I said. I've been walking for a couple of hours.

You must be cold.

Yes, I am, I replied.

Well, look, you might as well come in for a while. I can at least make you a cup of coffee.

I'd appreciate that, I said and followed him into the house.

So where you headed? he asked, leading me into a store-room under the stairs with a sink, a table and two folding chairs.

I've been thinking about going to New York City, I said.

Thinking about? he asked, filling a kettle with water from a filtering system attached to the faucet.

Well, that was the original plan. But I'm not so sure any-more, I said.

Where you from?

Round Bay, California, I answered.

That's quite a ways away.

I know it is, I said.

So you're just driving around.

Sort of.

Trying to find yourself, he went on.

Something like that.

Well, that's admirable, he said. I think it's good for people your age to take some time and experience life before going to college.

Actually, I never really thought about going to college, I said.

Really?

Doesn't run in the family. Besides, I could never afford it.

It *is* expensive, he said.

It's hard enough to get a job these days.

Ya, your generation's got a lot to compete against, he said. Your parents were luckier that way. Country was still young. Lots of work to be had. That's when a degree actually meant something. Now things are so specialized. Just when you get the hang of things, they become obsolete. That's the way it is with computers at any rate.

I wouldn't know about that, I said.

I did my degree in electrical engineering, then I got into computers for a while. I've still got one, mind you, Macintosh Classic, but it's impossible to keep up with all the new technology.

Have you always lived here?

No, he said. My wife and I moved back here in '82, to get away from the bullshit of the big city. We wanted to feel like we belonged to a community and this way, with the store, that is, we still get to meet new people all the time, but under more personal circumstances. Do you take milk?

Yes, please.

Sugar?

No, thanks, I said and cupped my hands around the warm mug.

So you think your car is a few miles down the road?

At least, I said.

Do you know what's wrong with it?

No, I said. It just lost all its power.

Hm, he said. What kind of a car is it?

Dodge Omni.

Nope, that doesn't sound good to me.

I haven't got that much money, I said.

So you're in a bit of a jam, then.

I sighed and finished off the coffee. I looked down at my wet shoes on the hardwood floor.

Look, I've got to go do some errands right now, but I can leave you on the porch. There's a sofa out there, and a sleeping bag. You can catch a few winks before my wife wakes up. I'll call and let her know. I've got a friend who's a mechanic. I'll see what he can do for you.

Thanks, I said. I wasn't sure what I was gonna do.

Well, you came to the right place. We'll try and help you out, he said, taking my mug and putting it into the sink. Come with me, he said and I followed him through the store, back out to the porch. He took an old brown nylon sleeping bag out of a trunk and unrolled it on the sofa. It was lined with flannelette. The material was well worn and I could just make out the traces of a faded pattern of World War One fighter planes. You'll be fine here, he said and raised his eyebrows . . .

John, I said. John Wade.

I'm Salvator Shapiro, he said. Salamander to some, but feel free to call me Sal. I'll see you in a few hours.

Thanks, I said again. I really appreciate this.

Don't worry about it. It's good karma, he said and left the porch. I heard him get into his van and start the engine, then the tires crunching down on the gravel as he backed out of the drive. I heard him shift into second and accelerate.

I took my jacket off and hung it over the back of a chair. I unzipped my jeans and pulled them down. I laid them across the chair, then peeled my underwear off and my t-shirt. I picked up the sleeping bag and stepped into it. I sat down on the sofa and looked around. There was a rug on the floor made from a long braided rope coiling out from the centre. There was a lamp on a small round table to the left and, taped to the wall, a child's drawing of a dog or a horse, I couldn't quite tell. I swung my legs up and leaned back. I stared at the beams on the ceiling, listening to the run-off land in that puddle beside the porch steps. I curled up into a ball, pulled the sleeping bag over my head and tucked it in, trapping the heat inside. The sofa was soft and I sank down into the gap between the cushions and the back rest and fell asleep.

I felt as if someone was watching me. I could even feel the soft heat of someone's breath on my face. I listened and could hear voices and people moving around inside the store. I slowly opened my eyes, just a crack, and saw a little mouth in front of me and smooth, milky skin, the kind of skin that only children have.

Come here, Jack, I heard a woman say. Leave him alone, he's tired.

But he's been asleep all day, the boy said.

Well, I guess he needs it.

How's he doing? I heard Sal say.

Well, he's tired, the poor kid.

I looked through his wallet, Sal went on. He's got twenty bucks and a California driver's license. Not much else. Half a two-dollar bill.

I wanna wake him up, the boy said.

Not yet, the woman said.

We'll get him up for dinner, Sal said. Then he can go back to bed if he needs to.

I'll just throw his clothes into the washing machine, the

woman said and I heard her walk over to the chair and fumble round in my pockets. I heard her put my car keys and some spare change down on the chair, then walk over to the door. I heard her whisper to the boy and footsteps and then the door close. I opened my eyes.

It was bright outside beyond the screens. I could see the tops of trees ruffling in the breeze against a clear blue sky. The air was warm and I was sweating in the sleeping bag. I listened to the noise the bugs were making, the soft tock as they hit the screen and the loud buzzing as they crawled along the wire mesh, trying to find a way in. I stretched and rolled over. My body was still humming with sleep, my muscles still tingling, so I pulled the bag back over my head and fell asleep again.

I felt a hand on my shoulder. John? Are you awake? It's six o'clock.

I opened my eyes and looked up into Sal's beaming face.

Evening, he said. Sleep well?

Yes, thanks, I said, sitting up.

Here, he said, handing over my freshly laundered clothes. Kaleigh washed them for you.

Thanks, I said.

She threw out your Marlboros. They were soggy anyways, but we don't like cigarette smoke in the house. The rest of your things are on the chair.

Thanks.

Dinner's in about ten minutes if you want to join us.

That'd be great, I said, realizing how hungry I was.

We're upstairs when you're ready. Just come on up, he said and went back into the store.

I picked up my t-shirt and brought it to my face. It smelt fresh and clean and the cotton was soft and white. I buried my nose in it then slipped it over my head. I got dressed inside the sleeping bag and stood up. I strolled over to the edge of the porch and looked out onto the backyard. There was a tire swing hanging from a tree and the grass was a vivid, electric green.

I slipped my wallet back into my pocket and went through the door into the health food store. To my immediate right was a kind of alcove full of soaps and shampoos next to a door marked PRIVATE. Further on, the store widened into three aisles for food. To the left, past the storeroom, was a long pinewood counter with a cash register. Behind the counter was a staircase leading up to another door. I walked up the stairs and knocked softly and stepped inside. Hello? I said, and a little boy came running out of a room and down the hall. Jeronimo! he screamed, waving a plastic sword and stabbing me in the leg. His smile was contagious and I reached out and touched his curly light brown hair with my fingertips.

I saw you sleeping, he said suddenly.

I know, I said.

How do you know if you were asleep? he asked.

I was peeking, I said.

Were not, he said.

Was so.

I got a telescope for my birthday. Wanna see it?

Not right now, his mother said, coming down the hall towards me. Hi, John. I'm Kaleigh. And this is our son, Jack, she said, holding out her hand. He just had a birthday.

I'm six, Jack said, crossing his arms without letting go of his sword.

It's nice to meet you, Kaleigh said. You had a rough night last night, I hear.

I've had better, I said. Thanks for washing my clothes.

No problem, she said. Are you hungry?

I'm starving, I said and followed her down the hall and into the kitchen. The kitchen was painted a burnt orange with glossy white mouldings. The window above the sink was steamed up and the sill crowded with plants. There was an old-fashioned table pushed up against the wall to the left of the door, with four wooden chairs pushed in around it. The kitchen smelt of freshly baked bread.

Kaleigh was almost as tall as Sal, only slimmer, and had long blonde hair that hung in a loose braid down her back. She was wearing a thin sweater over a cotton dress and her arms and legs were lightly tanned. Her face was broad and friendly and she exuded a calm confidence. She possessed that ageless, healthy, all-American type of beauty, but I figured she was around the same age as Sal. Sal was sitting at the table reading the paper, but when he saw me walk in he looked up and flashed me a grin. He put the paper down and pulled Jack onto his lap.

I nodded back to him and pulled out a chair. The table was set for dinner and Kaleigh took a bowl of potato salad out of the fridge and handed it to Sal. She placed a warm loaf of brown bread onto a cutting board and Sal cut four thick slices and flopped one onto every plate. Kaleigh then placed a pot of cold vegetable soup, something she called Gazpacho, onto the table and started ladling it into four blue glass bowls. Jack sat on a phone book on the chair beside me, looked up and pulled a face.

I called my mechanic friend today, Sal said, buttering his bread, and he's coming over with his tow-truck this evening to fetch your car. Then we can have a look at it and see what the damage is.

That would be great, I said. This is really nice of you.

Well, I did a bit of travelling when I was your age, he said. Lots of people helped me out. People I never saw again. I'm only returning the favour, as I hope you'll do one day if you're in the position to. You know what they say, what goes around comes around. Well, what comes around should also go round too. I think it's good to even the balance.

When's Nate coming round? Kaleigh asked. Should I save him some dinner?

Well, you know Nate, Sal answered.

Can I show John my bedroom? Jack asked.

Not right now, Kaleigh said.

After dinner?

I think he's gonna be too busy this evening. They've got to go get his car.

Did he smash it up?

Why don't you ask him yourself. He's right there, Kaleigh said.

Jack suddenly went all shy and hid his face behind his hands, peeking out occasionally to look at his mother. Go on, she said. You can ask him.

I didn't have a crash, I said to the backs of Jack's pudgy hands. It wasn't nearly that exciting. The engine lost all its power and I just drifted to the side of the road.

My dad's gonna teach me how to drive when I turn fourteen, Jack said, losing his shyness as quickly as he'd acquired it.

You're lucky, I said, and he grew serious, his forehead gathering in a little knot between his eyebrows.

Where's your dad? he asked.

I think he's still in California, I said.

Don't you know for sure?

I haven't spoken to him for a long time, I said and saw Kaleigh turn to look at Sal out of the corner of my eye.

Come on, Jack, she said. Finish up your soup, sweetheart.

But it's yucky, he said.

It'll put hairs on your chest, Sal said.

I don't want hairs on my chest, Jack said, wrinkling his nose in disgust.

Well, how about a beard then? Sal asked and stroked his chin. Just like mine.

Jack gave his dad an exasperated look and started rocking back and forth in his chair. Come on, Kaleigh said. Hurry up now, before your soup gets cold, and Jack swung his head around and looked at her intently.

Mom-my, he said and she smiled at him. It's supposed to be cold.

Sal laughed and reached over and poked Jack in the stomach. He squirmed out of his chair, jumped down and ran out of the kitchen.

After dinner, Jack took me to his bedroom. There was a faded quilt on his bed and paintings on the walls that he'd obviously done himself. The one that caught my eye was of a house with a red door, and two people joined at the hands standing beside a tree with a tire swing dangling from a branch. Someone had painted *I love mommy and daddy* inside a cloud in the sky. In another cloud they'd written *me*, and painted an arrow to the swing. I looked closer and saw a small pink smudge perched on top of the black tire.

Is that you? I asked, pointing to the blotch of paint.

Yes, he said. When I was a baby.

Oh, I said and he pulled me over to the window.

This is a Splinter, he said, pointing to a furry cactus in a small clay pot on the windowsill. I'm not allowed to touch it with my fingers because it's prickly. Mom says the prickles feel like splinters. I got a splinter once, when I was carrying wood for my dad, right here on this finger, he said holding up his second finger for me to see.

Ouch, I said.

You can't see it anymore, he said. It doesn't hurt.

Well, that's good.

Wanna see my telescope?

I nodded and he lifted the lid of a small red treasure chest on the floor by the radiator and pulled out a brand-new telescope, twelve inches long and metallic grey. It looked quite heavy and had an adjustable tripod attached to the wide end. There's not much to see during the daytime, he said. My favourite planet is Mars because it's red and fiery.

It's easy to find, isn't it? I said.

It's the fourth one from the sun. Do you know how I know that?

No, I said, smiling down at him.

My dad taught me a sentence so I could remember all the

planets. My very excellent mother just served us nine pizzas.

That's a good way to remember, I said and heard the door-bell ring downstairs.

That must be Nate, Jack said. You don't know him but he's a friend of the family. He can fix anything.

That's good, I said. 'Cause I'm gonna need all the help I can get.

Nathan looked the part. He was wearing a baseball cap over a small dark ponytail, his jeans were smeared with grease and his hands and fingernails were black.

I'll give you a kiss, Kaleigh was saying as we came down the hall. As long as you keep your hands off me, Nate.

You sure do like to make a man suffer, he said, raising his hands in the air.

Don't be silly, she said, giggling and giving him a kiss on the cheek.

So is this the young man? he asked, nodding in my direction, taking Jack into a headlock and rubbing the top of his head with his knuckles.

Ya, Kaleigh said. John, this is Nathan. Mechanic and self-professed bachelor.

To the bitter end, he said.

I really appreciate you helping me out, I said.

Don't worry about it. The only thing I can fault you for so far is buying an Omni in the first place. Shit cars. Major structural flaws.

I didn't know that, I said.

I heard a toilet flush and Sal came down the hall, buttoning up his fly. Hey there, Nate. How's the Carrera coming along?

Good, he said.

I should hope so with all the money you've been sinking into it.

She's worth it though.

The way you talk about that car, Kaleigh said, you'd think you were referring to your girlfriend.

She's better than that. Never tires of letting me get inside her.

You're disgusting, she said, rolling her eyes and covering Jack's ears with her hands.

Meet John? Sal asked.

Yah, I already introduced them, Kaleigh said.

Well, we might as well head off now while there's still some daylight left.

But I just got here, Nathan protested.

You can put your feet up when we get back, Sal said, and he headed down the stairs.

We piled into the cab of Nathan's tow-truck and drove down the road in the direction I had come from. We crossed the bridge over what Sal told me was Little Trout river and started up the hill. A few minutes later, we drove past the barrier on the opposite side of the road where I had stopped the night before. I sat squeezed up against the door, listening to the men talk. Nathan was telling Sal about the customized parts he was having to order from a dealer that specialized in foreign cars, and how much they were costing him. Sal repeated what Kaleigh had said earlier, saying that if Nathan even half-loved a woman the way he loved that car, he'd be a happily married man by now.

Well, hell, Nathan said. I don't see anything wrong with it.

It's like hormone replacement therapy, Sal said. It ain't the real thing, baby.

I don't know what the real thing is anymore, Nathan said.

You gotta bring a child into the world to know that, Sal said, and they both went quiet.

Nathan finally broke the silence by saying that Sal was unforgivably middle class and that he'd sold out years ago. I didn't know exactly what Nathan meant by that, but Sal just laughed and shrugged it off.

They continued to talk in the easy, jocular manner of men who've known each other for a long time, maybe even witnessed each others' weaknesses or mistakes, as if compassion was measured in direct proportion to how hard they were on each other. They were like two old men fishing off a bridge, or driving back from a hunting trip with a deer strapped to the hood of the car. They seemed to be flexing their muscles constantly as they talked.

Nathan leaned forward over the wheel and looked at me, So how far did you walk last night, John?

I'm not sure, I said. Took me a few hours, I think. It was dawn by the time I got to Bridgewater.

Nathan raised his eyebrows and his mouth drooped at the corners. We drove on for another twenty minutes or so. I kept my eyes peeled, searching the far shoulder until finally, after a bend in the road, I caught sight of my little Dodge Omni, parked exactly where I had left it, like a dog waiting for its master's return.

There it is, I said.

Land ho! Nathan bellowed, then checked the odometer.

[183]

You walked just under twelve miles last night, John.

Really?

No wonder you slept all day, Sal said, leaning forward and eyeing my car as we slowed down to a stop.

Nathan glanced over his shoulder then did a U-turn in the road. He pulled over in front of my car and reversed, parking a few feet away from my front bumper. We got down from the tow-truck and Nathan went over and raised the hood and peered inside. He scratched his cheek then walked around to the passenger side. He squatted down, spun his baseball cap round backwards and leant forward until he was on all fours and his face was nearly touching the ground. After a while he straightened up, went back to the truck and started letting out the cable. He placed a rubber padded sling under the front end of the car and threaded the chains through the front axle. He attached the hook to the sling and started to reel in the cable. Sal walked over to the driver's seat, put his hands up to the glass and peered inside, looking first into the front, then into the back, as the whole front end of the vehicle began to lift into the air.

Did you drink all that booze? he asked, coming back over to where I was standing.

No, I said, remembering that I hadn't thrown out any of the empty cans or bottles since Hannah left. I was travelling with a friend for a while, I went on, motioning with my hand as if that was all behind me now. Haven't had a drink since.

Where did your friend go?

Don't know, I said. She just left one day.

Just like that?

Guess she'd had enough of my company, I said, trying to smile and be flippant about the whole thing.

[184]

You've had a pretty rough time, haven't you?

No worse than some, I said.

Feel like you're over it?

There was nothing to get over, I said.

I mean about the booze, he said.

Oh that, I said.

You don't have a drinking problem, do you?

What? I asked. At my age?

I can trust you then, can I?

I looked at him. I felt my chest heave and let out a deep breath. Yes, I said. That was all I wanted.

Sal patted me on the shoulder then walked to the front of the car. Everything OK here? he asked Nathan.

Ya, just about ready, he answered, straightening up.

Nathan made sure the car was secure, then we got back into the truck and drove off. The sun was sinking into the hills and a cool blanket of shade had descended over the valley. We pulled into the parking lot of the health food store and I opened the door and stepped down. I followed Sal up the stairs and into the kitchen. Kaleigh was sitting at the table, staring at her hands.

What's up? Sal said.

Just lost in thought, she said, shaking her head and sitting up straight.

Jack in bed?

Yep. You want some tea? she asked me.

Sure, I said and sat down in the corner so that I was out of the way. Sal left the kitchen while Kaleigh filled the kettle. Nathan came in and went over to the sink and started scrubbing his hands with soap.

How come I can never work up a good lather in this house? he said, rubbing his hands together.

Kaleigh laughed. You're doing it right now, Nate.

What? he asked.

Working yourself into a lather.

You know what I mean, he said.

It's allergen free, she said. Doesn't contain any lauryl sulfate, which is what makes things lather. Some people are allergic to it.

Ya, well I'm not, he said. I like a little lather.

I know you do, Kaleigh said and reached up to get some mugs out of the cupboard.

I sat at the table and waited to hear what Nathan had to say about my car. He hadn't offered an opinion and I didn't want to pester him seeing as he was already doing me a favour. Sal came back into the kitchen with a little wooden box the size of a mouse trap and put it down on the table. He took off his jacket and hung it over the back of his chair, sat down and rolled up his sleeves. He slid the top off the wooden box and took out a small plastic bag.

You read my mind, Nathan said, wiping his hands on a dishtowel and joining us at the table. Sal took some weed out of the bag and started cutting off little bits of the furry red-green bud with a tiny pair of nail scissors. He broke the pieces up with his fingers, then pulled out a rollie and flattened it down, using the top flap of a pack of matches to shovel the grass onto the paper. He picked it up, rubbed the ends between his fingers, tucked the bottom in, licked the glue and rolled it shut. He made a filter out of an old hockey card that was in the box, turned the joint around and baptized it. After he'd lit up, Sal dabbed some more spit around the end so that it would burn evenly. He took a long haul, then passed the spliff to Nathan. Nathan took a drag then passed it to me, still holding the smoke in his lungs. I inhaled and heard a seed pop, then passed it to Kaleigh. She took a toke and sat down. It was as if a collective sigh had descended on the kitchen. Nobody said anything until the ritual was over and Sal got up to run some tap water over the roach. He opened the cupboard under the sink and threw it into the garbage can.

Just what the doctor ordered, Sal said, clapping his hands together and lifting the tea-cozy off a pot of tea. This ready? he asked Kaleigh and put the tea-cozy on his head.

She turned to look at him over her shoulder and started to laugh. You look like a bishop, she said, and Sal raised his hand vertically and moved it in circles in the air.

Maybe you could say a prayer for John's car, Nathan said.

Ah yes, John's car, Sal said, taking the tea-cozy off his head. So what's the prognosis, doctor?

I'm not sure, Nathan said, turning to me. I'm gonna have to take a better look at it. It could be the timing belt. The timing belts on Omnis are always snapping. Could be the electrics, the carburettor, who knows?

Great, I said.

Well, I wouldn't exactly say great, Nathan said, chuckling to himself. Naw, that wouldn't be my word for it.

It's not funny, I pleaded.

You're right, Nathan said, holding in his breath. It's very, very serious.

How long will it take to fix? I asked.

I don't know yet. It might take a few days if I need to order parts. Then there's the labour . . .

And how much is it gonna cost? I asked.

More than you can afford, in my estimation, Sal said, taking a sip of his tea and licking his moustache. More than you got on you right now, that's for sure.

I leaned forward, dropped my head into my hands and sighed. I could hear Nathan and Kaleigh trying hard not to laugh, little explosions of breath, a slap on the knee, a whispered, Stop that!

I have an idea, Sal said at last.

I looked up and he was stroking his beard, staring up at the ceiling.

Maybe we can work something out. I've been meaning to hire someone to help out around the store, do inventory, clean up, that sort of thing, and if you promise to stay in line, you know, I'll give you the job in return for room and board, and a small salary, just until the car's been paid off. What do you think, Kaleigh?

Well, she said, lifting her hand and wiping the corner of her eye. I dunno. Where are we gonna put him?

He can sleep on the porch, Sal said.

It wouldn't be very comfortable.

I don't mind, I said.

Well, if you don't mind, Kaleigh said, I guess I don't have a problem with it.

You must be one hell of a lucky kid, Nathan said to me. To land here of all places. I don't know a lot of people who'd stick their necks out like these two here. You must have a horseshoe up your ass.

Oh, is that what it is, I said. I was beginning to wonder.

I think we're going to get along just fine, Sal said. Just fine.

When I woke up the next morning, Jack was sitting on the floor next to me, cutting out bits of coloured paper and pasting them onto a white background. Morning Jack, I said.

Mom said that if I was quiet and didn't wake you I could stay in here.

I don't mind, I said. What are you making?

It's for you, he said and covered it up with his hands.

I won't look, I said, and sat up. On the chair where I had laid my clothes out the night before were another pair of jeans, a pair of dark grey sweatpants, a couple of t-shirts and a sweatshirt. I reached over and picked up the sweatpants.

You can have those, Jack said. They're dad's, but he doesn't wear them anymore.

That's really nice of him, I said and held them up by the waist. I put them on inside my sleeping bag and stood up. They were a couple of sizes too big but fit well enough with the drawstring pulled tight. I put on a fresh t-shirt, then folded the sleeping bag and put it to one side. I smiled down at Jack, then opened the door to the store and ventured inside. A woman in slacks and sandals was reading the label on a bottle of shampoo inside the alcove to my right. She gave me a look, then put the bottle back on the shelf. I walked through to the checkout counter where Kaleigh was attending to a white-haired man buying a large bag of porridge oats.

Morning, John, she said, giving me a smile. I recognize those clothes.

[189]

Whaddya think?

Very nice, she said. Feel free to go upstairs and use the washroom if you want. Have a shower, whatever. There are towels in the hall closet and I put a new toothbrush in the cup. Yours is the red one, okay?

Thanks, I said. I won't be long.

When I returned downstairs, Kaleigh let out a whistle. You're a changed man, John. You look better when you're clean.

I feel better too, I said.

Sal came out of the storeroom and gave me a quick tour of the place. First he acquainted me with the kinds of things that were kept near the checkout counter. Impulse buys, he called them. Home-made cookies and date squares, high-energy snacks, sesame and granola bars, vitamin E and Badger Balm. He showed me where the breads were kept in the aisle closest to the door, next to the corn and kettle-baked potato chips. At the end of the aisle, running the length of the far wall, was a large fridge containing butter, milk, cheese, tofu and fresh organic juices.

Sal then led me to the bulk food section in the middle aisle, and identified the contents of every barrel. There was long and short grain rice, oats, four different types of beans, green and red lentils, unbleached flour and cornmeal. Above the barrels was a row of clear plastic dispensers containing raisins, dried apricots, bananas, trail mix and muesli, all of which needed refilling on a daily basis.

Finally, Sal took me into the alcove at the back of the store, past the door to the basement, and introduced me to all the different types of skin-care products. Next to a basket of loofa sponges was a row of books, self-help manuals and guides to vitamins and herbal remedies. On the wall, next to the back door, was a small shelf like a spice rack that contained an assortment of aromatherapy and essential oils.

It might seem like a lot to remember for now, but don't worry, Sal said. You'll get the hang of it in no time.

He led me into the storeroom and handed me a clipboard with a checklist of all the chores that needed to be done. All the products had to be taken off the shelves and the shelves cleaned at least once a week. The products on the bottom shelves had to be dusted and the bulk food section refilled when necessary. Due dates on items in the fridge had to be checked and the older products moved to the front. The floors had to be swept and mopped every day at closing time and, finally, an inventory had to be done every two days to see which products were selling and what needed to be reordered. By the time I'd read the whole list, I was completely put off. I hadn't had to work or discipline myself in years, and I couldn't for the life of me see how all this work was going to get done.

I think Sal must have seen the desperation in my face because he decided to give me a little break and left me alone in the storeroom. I just wanted to go back to sleep, but then I thought about everything he and Kaleigh were doing for me and steeled myself to the task. Sal popped his head around the corner to tell me he was taking Jack to a friend's house, and that Kaleigh wanted me to keep an eye on things while she went upstairs for a moment. I jumped up and followed him over to the cash. The store was relatively quiet and Kaleigh came down a few minutes later with two sandwiches and a couple of empty glasses. She went over to the fridge and took out a bottle of apple cider. She came over to the counter and filled the glasses.

A friend of ours makes this stuff, she said. You'll meet him one day, Elroy Deer. Owns an apple orchard near Harpersfield. It's all organic.

It's delicious, I said, taking a large sip.

Ya. He helped us a lot when we first opened up. Gave us a loan and everything. He and his wife have been like grandparents to Jack, but we don't see them as often as we used to.

He's a nice kid, I said.

Jack? Ya, we're very lucky.

You seem to have the perfect family.

Well, it's not always perfect, but we manage to survive. Sometimes Sal isn't the most attentive father, but I'm not complaining. He just gets distracted easily, which is not necessarily a bad thing because it's also what makes him a good entrepreneur. He doesn't shy away from taking risks. We wouldn't have the store otherwise. But how are you getting on?

There's so much to learn.

Don't let it intimidate you. After a while you'll know everything by heart. Everything from cod liver oil to evening primrose, she said, smiling and finishing off her apple cider.

You just seem to know so much.

Well, I have been in the business for six years. Ever since Jack was born.

He really is a wonderful kid.

Ya, we're very lucky, she said again.

*

That evening, after Jack had gone to bed and Kaleigh had retired with a book, Sal and I stayed up in the livingroom listening to music and eating popcorn. The livingroom walls were deep forest green, and there were two large brown corduroy sofas facing each other, piled high with pillows. There was an Oriental rug on the hardwood floor and a round coffee table with elaborate carved legs and a brass plate filled with oranges in the centre of the room. The walls were lined with books, and to my knowledge the Shapiros didn't own a TV set. There was a rubber plant the size of a small tree in the corner of the room, and a tiled fireplace full of powdery white ashes. I mentioned to Sal how badly I was craving a cigarette, so he offered to roll another joint.

You know, he said after a long, stoned silence, I've got a bit of a sideline going. Bit of a hobby, if you like, and I think it might help you quit smoking, assuming that you want to, that is.

I guess so, I said.

It's a kind of therapy, he went on, stroking his chin in a way that was becoming familiar to me. It's a form of meditation. In your case, it might be a good way to explore the roots of unwanted behaviour. Ya, come to think about it, this might be just what you need.

What is it? I asked.

It's gonna blow your mind, John, he said, leaning forward and clapping his hands together. Follow me, he said and gave me a wink.

We stood up and I followed him downstairs. We stopped in front of the door with the PRIVATE sign on it and Sal took out a set of keys. He unlocked the door and led me down into an unfinished basement. The floor and walls were rough and made of poured concrete. The ceiling was low and there was a single light bulb hanging in the centre of the room. To the left of the stairs was a standing shower stall with sliding doors next to a bench, a terry-towel bathrobe, a pair of white slippers, and two ten-pound dumbbells.

Weightlifting? I asked him. Is this what you brought me down here for?

Not quite, he said with a wry smile. Come over here.

We walked around behind the stairs and Sal reached up and switched on another bare light bulb. A purple egg-shaped container appeared before my eyes, about eight feet long by five feet high, and it looked to be completely sealed. I turned to Sal and he was beaming.

What in the world . . . I began to say but he cut me off.

Flotation tank, he said. This here is a self-contained, self-monitoring, fibreglass capsule. It's a beaut, don't you think? Seven hundred pounds of magnesium sulphate hepta-hydrate in a hundred and seventy gallons of water, creates a ten-inch deep solution which is heated to ninety-three point five degrees Fahrenheit, to match your skin temperature. Unless you're an astronaut, this is the only situation you will ever encounter in which your body is totally free from the forces of gravity.

God, I said.

Pretty impressive, isn't it.

How does it work?

You get inside.

And then what?

You float, kiddo. You just float. That's why it's called a flotation tank.

Right, I said.

It's a form of relaxation. So deep that it causes your body to release certain feel-good hormones. They're called endorphins, something like what you're feeling right now from the pot, only natural. With earplugs in, totally naked and in the dark, it's like being back in the womb.

And that's a good feeling, is it?

When women are pregnant, John, they produce up to eight times the natural levels of endorphins. So in the womb, babies are on a constant natural high. That's why it's so nice in there, and why it's such a traumatic experience when we're born, because we don't like it when that feeling comes to an end. Birth is like withdrawal. Life as re-hab. It's a pretty shitty beginning.

Right, I said. I can't remember that far back.

I bet you could if you tried. Lots of people have trauma connected to the birthing process, only it's buried under years of socializing. It's quite common to have a rebirthing experience in the tank, and it's hard, you know, but people are usually grateful for the opportunity, a chance to exorcize those very first negative emotions.

I dunno, I said.

Look, John, opening up is not always an uncomplicated or happy experience, but it's one I'm totally committed to. I'd like to start a business, you know, provide people with their own tanks at an affordable price.

I'm not so sure I'm up for this.

It's harmless, John. It's only water for chrissake. And warm water, at that. Trust me.

I looked at the tank, like some giant mutant eggplant lying

on the floor, then back at Sal. I took a deep breath and said, Okay, I'll try it.

Great, he said and pushed up the roll-top lid. He leaned in and switched some lights on inside the tank. I walked over and put my head inside and felt the heat and humidity on my face. I could smell the Epsom salt. Sal walked over to a card table set up in the corner of the room and picked something up. You'll need these, he said and handed me a pair of earplugs. They're clean, he said and went back over to the table. I heard him push the eject button on a tape deck and flip a tape.

Just a little music to get you into the mood, he said. Always helps me to focus. Now remember, John, the water is very salty. There's a bottle of fresh water hanging inside on the left in case you get any in your eyes. The light switch is also on the left. When you get comfortable, turn them off. And I recommend that you float with your hands about level with your head because it's more comfortable that way.

How long do I stay in for? I asked.

About an hour, Sal said and patted me on the back. He showed me how to lock the tank from the inside, then said, I'll let you get undressed.

I stopped him halfway up the stairs and said, What if I fall asleep?

Doesn't matter if you do, he said, looking at me through the wooden slats of the steps. An hour in the tank is worth four in bed.

What if I drown? I blurted out.

You can't drown in a flotation tank, John. The water holds

you up. Just let yourself go. You gotta trust me on this one, he said and climbed the stairs, leaving me alone with the purple orb.

I could hear the floorboards creak above me as Sal moved around the store. I twisted the earplugs in and untied my sweatpants. Looking around to make sure nobody was watching, I quickly pulled them down, slipped my t-shirt over my head and stepped into the tank. The bottom half was lined with smooth blue rubber. The water was warm and perfectly clear. I crouched down, pulled the hatch down and locked it. The lights underwater cast trembling shadows on the domed ceiling which was covered in tiny beads of condensation, like pearls embedded in the fibreglass.

I sat down in the water. It was like sitting down on the side of an inflatable dingy. The water was spongy and buoyant. It was hot in the tank, almost oppressive, and the air felt dense with vapour. I stretched my legs out and they popped to the surface like life jackets. I couldn't keep them down. It was a strange sensation. I reclined some more and my bum also popped to the surface so that my entire weight was being supported by my fingertips. I laid back and put my head in the water. I lifted my fingers off the bottom and felt suspended in air.

I have to admit, it was an incredible sensation.

I moved slowly like a turtle, arching my back to the left and then to the right. I moved my arms up and let out a long sigh. I could hear my heartbeat like a padded hammer in my ear. I closed my eyes and felt as if I was spinning, like when you step off a boat and still feel the roll of the waves beneath your feet. It was as if my body was used to compensating for a movement or a force that was no longer active, maybe it was gravity. Having lost the downward pull, I felt as if I was rising in the water.

Relieved of the responsibility of holding up my bones, I felt my muscles slip. I wasn't just floating, I was levitating on the water. I felt exhilarated and reached up to my left and switched the lights off. All the colour vanished. Nothing but blackness and for a moment I panicked. I sat up and noticed three thin cylinders of light, hanging like stalactites from the ceiling near my feet. I reached up and felt three small air holes in the fibreglass top. I moved my thumb aside and the light came shooting down like solid poles. I moved my arm and watched the bright spots travel like coins across my skin. I lay back down. In the darkness, the tank could have been as huge as a cathedral. There were no edges. No beginnings and no ends.

I must have drifted off to sleep because when I woke the music was off and someone was in the tank with me, a woman, underneath me, trying to push her way up to the surface. I could feel her hands pressing into my back and heard her distant voice calling out to me. I had to get out of the way but the tank had shrunk, it was no larger than a coffin and I couldn't move aside to let her up. My body was like a lid she was trying to pry open. The more I tried to move the more the walls squeezed in on me. Her voice was faint but she continued to call out my name.

John! she shouted. John! It's me, Kaleigh. Unhook the latch, John. Can you hear me? John! she shouted. Wake up!

Kaleigh went on pounding the side of the tank while I wrenched myself back from dreaming. I was shivering in the heat and my teeth were chattering. I sat up and switched on the light. I got on my knees and slid the door open. There was a rush of cold air. I looked up and saw Kaleigh's worried face in front of me. John, are you okay?

I pulled the earplugs out.

Are you okay? she asked again.

Yes, I said.

Are you sure?

I'm freezing, I said, and she walked over to the shower and picked up the robe and brought it back.

Sal came to bed, she said. I stayed up to finish my book and I was just about to fall asleep when I remembered that you were down here.

What time is it? I asked.

You've been in for nearly two hours, she said. When you didn't answer, I dunno. I'm just glad you're alright.

I stood up and she wrapped the robe around me and rubbed my upper arms like I was a child.

There was lots of work to do around the Appleseed Emporium. Sal kept me so busy that time passed swiftly. A steady flow of menial tasks kept my mind off other things and I took a certain satisfaction in my job. At the end of the day, I felt content in a way I hadn't been since my boyhood days in Round Bay.

On one particularly warm evening, after I'd swept and mopped the floor, I went out to the backyard and sat down on the grass. Evening shadows were sloping across the lawn and the air was full of pollen. I raised my face to the sun and felt the warmth on my skin. I picked at a blister on the inside of my thumb, tearing the loose skin and draining the water. If time had stood still then and trapped me forever in that pool of hot sunshine, I think I would have been a happy man. The screen door opened and Sal came over and stood beside me.

Beautiful evening, isn't it?

Hm, I agreed, nodding my head. I leant forward and rested my elbows on my knees and looked at my hands. I could feel a vein under my skin throbbing in time to my heart.

We've got a friend coming round for dinner, he said. Thought we'd roast some red peppers on the barbecue. You're welcome to join us.

I'd like that, I said and heard the van on the gravel and Kaleigh pulled up near the grass. Jack got out and stooped to inspect something on the ground. Kaleigh waved, then went into the house.

Later on, I helped Sal carry some chairs out to the lawn. Kaleigh arranged the food on an old wool blanket, while I pushed Jack on the tire swing and Sal lit the barbecue. I looked over when I heard footsteps on the driveway and a woman rounded the house, carrying a bowl sealed tight with Saran-Wrap. I gave Jack an extra-strong push and walked over to meet her.

This is Mary-Beth, Kaleigh said, standing next to her and giving the woman a sideways hug. Mary-Beth was a small, delicate-boned woman with short brown hair, freckled skin and startling blue eyes like the eyes of an arctic Husky. She was wearing shorts and tennis shoes and a bright red blouse tied at the waist.

Nice to meet you, she said. John, isn't it?

That's right, Kaleigh said, and we shook hands. Where's maudlin?

Oh, she's coming, Mary-Beth said, rolling her eyes. She's looking for hemlock by the side of the road.

Kaleigh laughed. And poison ivy, I bet.

If it was up to her, it'd be Halloween every day of the year. I swear I don't know where she gets it from. Sometimes I think they must've switched babies at the hospital. I keep hoping it's just a phase.

I'm sure it is, Kaleigh said. At least you know she's smart.

I'll give her that. All she does is read. She already knows more about herbal medicine than I ever will know.

Well, there you go. What did you bring?

It's a new recipe, she said. Almond and artichoke salad.

Another one of Maude's concoctions?

Sure is.

She's so funny, Kaleigh said, and I heard more footsteps on the gravel, slower this time and dragging.

Speak of the devil, Mary-Beth said, as a short, pale-skinned girl came round the corner of the house. She was younger than I expected and still had the round plumpness of a little girl.

Heya, Maude, Sal called extra cheerfully. Over here.

Maude raised her face and looked up. Her cheeks were flushed and she looked hot in her black jeans and black sweatshirt. A few strands of long black hair were stuck to her damp forehead.

Hello, she said glumly.

Find any hemlock? Mary-Beth asked.

Mo-ther, she said and walked over to the barbecue. Sal handed her the tongs and gave her control of the red peppers. Maude prodded the charred black skins then started to poke the coals, sending smoke signals up into the air. She rolled up the sleeve of her sweatshirt, revealing a milky white forearm.

How old is she? I whispered to Kaleigh.

She's only eleven, Kaleigh said. But well beyond her years.

Kaleigh knelt down and peeled the plastic wrap off the bowl Mary-Beth had brought. Dig in folks, she said, and I sat down beside her on the edge of the blanket.

Jack ran over from the swing and stood by Maude at the barbecue. He tried to get her attention by staring up at her, but she refused to acknowledge his presence. She ignored him long enough to bore him and he eventually came over and sat down in my lap. It was the first time he'd done that and his little body was warm and lively in my lap. I felt a mixture of tenderness and arousal. I put my hands around his waist to lift him to one side, but he squealed and wriggled out of my grip. His hands and feet kept pressing into my crotch, so I shifted his bum over to my left leg and held him there. I'm not going to tickle you, I said.

Sit still, sweetie, Kaleigh said. Or come over here. John wants to have his dinner.

Jack shook his head and settled down on my lap. Kaleigh handed out the plates and asked Maude to serve the peppers. When she came around, she dropped a pepper on my plate without making eye contact and I wondered whether she was shy of me.

After dinner, I stretched out on the grass, quietly digesting, feeling the cooling air on my arms and legs, listening to the bees like electric shavers trimming the pollen from the flowers. The adults were playing a word game and I only half-listened, lying on my back with my head on my arms. The evening softened into night, even softened Maude's sharp edges and she consented to play with Jack, lying on her back and lifting him into the air on the bottom of her feet. After a while, she came over and sat down beside me.

Hi, I said, but she didn't answer me. So what grade you in? I asked, trying to make conversation.

I'm on my summer holidays, she said.

Of course, I answered.

But I start highschool in the fall, she said after a while.

Looking forward to it? I asked, trying to remember my first day in junior high.

No, she said. I hate school. It's full of dunces.

Really?

The people in my class last year were so stupid. I had this teacher, Mrs Doyle. She was like sixty years old. Way too old to teach. I can't believe they still let her.

Well, you'll have more than one teacher in highschool.

I know, Maude said.

And you'll meet new people.

Who cares, she said.

And boys . . .

Boys are stupid.

They can't all be that bad, I suggested.

You don't know the boys I know. All they do is fart in class and goof off. They're always bugging the girls.

That's because they like them, I said.

Well, I don't know how anyone could find them attractive.

You'll like them soon enough.

That's what everybody keeps on telling me. I'm not interested, she said. I want to be a science-fiction writer. I won't have time for boys.

You'll make time for them, trust me.

I will not, she said. Why does everyone keep telling me how I'm gonna be? How do you know what I'm gonna be like? Nobody here understands. I can't wait till I'm old enough and can leave this place. I hate this town. It's so small. You need a regional map to find this place. My mom has a road map of New York State and we're not even on it. That's how unimportant we are, can you believe it? I don't even know why you want to stay here. If I was from California, I'd get in my car and drive back right this minute.

Ya, but I don't wanna go back, I said.

Anywhere is better than here.

That's not true, I said. It's great here. It's so peaceful.

It's boring here. I'm bored out of my tree. Nothing ever happens. Nobody ever comes to visit. Why would you want to stay here?

Well, I don't really have anywhere else to go.

Don't you have a family?

Not really.

Are you like an orphan or somethin'? she asked.

I guess so, I said. Kind of.

I'd like to be an orphan.

No, you wouldn't.

Yes, I would. Then I wouldn't have to stay anywhere I didn't want to, she said, ripping off a blade of grass and holding it between her thumbs. She brought it up to her mouth and blew on it. It made a noise like an antique car horn.

I rolled onto my stomach and watched Kaleigh get up from her chair and carry the dishes back into the house. She came out again with a pot of tea on a tray and six mugs. I sat up to drink my tea in the fading light. I saw a firefly flicker on and off in the blackberry bushes at the bottom of the garden. Another one appeared and eventually the brambles were swarming with fireflies, darting back and forth, like shooting stars.

Look, Sal said, pulling Jack to his side. The fairies are coming out.

After work the next day, I asked Sal if I could do another float. He told me I should make use of the tank whenever I wanted and showed me where he kept the spare key to the basement. He showed me how to use the heating system and turn on the filters. He left me downstairs and I got undressed. I slipped into the tank and closed the hatch. I turned the lights out right away and lay back in the warm, salty darkness. I let my mind slip out of focus and waited to see what would happen next. My thoughts wandered back to Round Bay and I tried to remember what Anna looked like, but in place of her eyes, I saw Hannah's. Instead of her mouth, I saw Hannah's mouth, her nose, her hair, her hands, all of it came rushing back to me. Even the dark triangle of her pubic hair was far more real to me than anything I could remember about Anna and I felt utterly alone then. Abandoned even by my memory. My chest felt hollowed out and empty. Filled only with the sound of my automatic heart continuing to beat because that's all it knew how to do.

I switched the lights back on and sat up. I got out of the tank, towelled down and went upstairs.

That was quick, Sal said, looking up from a notebook and nudging his glasses further up his nose.

Ya, I couldn't really get into it today.

Never mind, he said. Sometimes the magic works, sometimes it doesn't. I've got to go pick something up at Nate's in a minute. Wanna tag along? You could check the progress on the car front.

Sure, I said. Why not?

Nathan lived ten minutes off the main road, in a weathered old house that was in need of more than just a paint job. One of the upstairs windows was broken and boarded up and part of the chimney had crumbled away. Sal parked on the road, next to Nathan's tow-truck, and we got out of the van. There was a two-car garage to the left of the house with both doors wide open. Tires and auto parts spilled out in front like the whole building had been tilted forward and the contents tipped out. Old discarded hubcaps had been nailed to the walls so that the garage looked like a boy scout's hat covered in merit badges and souvenir pins. There was a rusty Volkswagen bug in the front yard that had been stripped down to its frame and propped up on bricks. Leaning up against the front porch like solar energy panels were lengths of aluminum sheeting. Sal called out a greeting and Nathan emerged, wiping his hands on a rag.

Hey there, Salamander. What's up?

I got an axe to grind with you.

Oh yeah, I forgot about that, didn't I? Nathan said, slapping his forehead.

I'd like it back if you're finished with it.

Only if you axe nicely, Nathan said and Sal groaned. Wait here and I'll go get it.

Nathan went into the garage and came out with a red-handled axe. Thanks, Sal said. But I was only kindling.

Nathan pretending to take a swing at Sal. That joke oughtta be taken out and shot, he said.

Given the axe, Sal said.

Enough already, Nathan said and handed it over.

So, how's the Omni coming along? Sal asked.

Well, Nathan said, turning and addressing me. I took it down to the shop and left it there. I was right about the timing belt. It just snapped, so I ordered one of those, and a new water pump 'cause yours was leaking. I wanna test the battery too. You might've just run it down, but it's pretty weak. I'll get back to you when that's all done.

Great, I said.

You two wanna beer or somethin'? Nathan asked.

Nah, Sal said. Gotta get back to the wife and kid.

Ah, the joys of married life.

You'll get lucky one of these days, Sal said.

That's not the kind of luck I'm looking for, Nathan said and winked at me. You wanna stay behind? I can drop you off on the way to my sister's.

Sure, I said. Why not?

Well, I'll be off then, Sal said and headed over to the van. See you back at the ranch, kiddo.

Sal drove off and I looked at Nathan.

I got something to show you, he said, and I followed him around behind the garage over to a car lying underneath a grey canvas tarp. Nathan went over and lifted the corner of the tarp like he was lifting a woman's skirt, then flung the whole thing aside in one exaggerated motion, revealing a slick, dark green sports car. Whaddya think?

It's nice, I said.

Nice? he replied. Do you have any idea what this little baby's worth? Nine eleven Carrera. Flat six cylinder engine, horizontally opposed, if that means anything to you. Fuel-injected, original leather interior, air-conditioning, flared fenders and a whale tail spoiler.

I gave him a blank look and shrugged my shoulders.

Pearls before swine, he said, shaking his head and taking a handkerchief out of his pocket. He bent over and breathed on the hood, then wiped the area clean. He stood back, tilted his head admiringly, then stooped to pick up the canvas tarp. Wanna give me a hand? he said and I picked up the other end. After we'd laid it gently over the car, Nathan rubbed his hands together and said, Wanna beer?

I dunno, I said.

Come on, he urged. I won't tell mom and dad.

It's not that, I said.

Let me guess. You're a nasty drunk. Well so am I, but I promise I won't drink too much. I've put in a good day's work and I think I deserve a beer. Besides, it'd be a sin not to drink on a day like this.

Nathan went into the house and I sat down on a rusty swing set in the backyard. He came out carrying two bottles of beer and leaned against the frame and the whole thing shifted sideways a couple of inches.

Cigarette? he asked, pulling a pack out of the front pocket of his overalls.

Oh God, yes, I said, taking one and bending forward into his lighter. I took a long drag and leaned back, my head reeling from the hit.

Let me guess. They've gotten you to give up smoking as well.

Sal's offered to roll me a joint whenever I have a craving, I said between puffs.

Ya, he had me on that diet for a while too. The thing is, he's just not a smoker. He doesn't understand how someone could prefer a simple cigarette. It's not the same. Sometimes you don't want to get fucked up, you just want to relax.

Exactly, I confirmed.

He's got a bad memory, does Sal. Can't remember shit about the old days. Pretends they never existed. Way back, before he moved away to do his degree, when we were about your age, back in the seventies, we used to cruise all over the state, going to bars, checking out the chicks. I'm telling you, Sal was a real womanizer back then, before he met the missus and embraced monogamy in a big way. Don't get me wrong, I love the woman. I love both of them. They're like family to me. I just can't stand to hear him pontificate like some bloody health food preacher. Like he's got all the answers. What I wouldn't give for a real hard-core blow-out. I'd like to see him lose it for a while, just to reassure myself, shake hands with the old Sal again, make sure he hasn't left us for good.

I guess having a kid changes all that, I said.

You got that right, Nathan said. I wouldn't know. Probably never will either. I already missed my chance.

Whaddya mean?

I had this girlfriend once. Her name was Rebecca. Beautiful woman and smart too. Don't know how I ever ended up with a woman like that, he said flicking his butt onto the grass. I was twenty-four and she was nineteen. The future was in the palm of our hands, or so I thought, but things got fucked up. Our wires got crossed somewhere along the line. We ended up wanting different things. She got pregnant, you see? And I made her all sorts of promises. I was gonna get a job, buy a house for us to live in. I thought things were gonna work out. I mean, I was happy. I was in love. I had a beautiful girl and she was gonna have my baby. The dream, it was all there. Then she got this letter in the mail. She got accepted into Cornell University. Ironically enough, it was Sal's suggestion. He was going in the fall and suggested she apply. She didn't think she had a hope in hell, so when she heard she'd been accepted, it was a real coup, you know? An ego boost. Boosted her right out of her senses. Suddenly, I guess, I didn't seem so important anymore. She went to her parents' place for dinner one evening, to tell them the news, you know, and the next time I saw her, well, she wasn't pregnant anymore. She didn't even ask my permission. Just went ahead and did it, without any regard for my feelings or anything. And that's just how it is. There are some things men and women simply don't share. At the end of the day, it's their baby. You don't really come into the picture while they're pregnant, not until you can hold the baby yourself. Until you start contributing your pay cheques. Hell, I don't begrudge it. That's just the way it is. It's a pretty shitty job having a kid. Morning sickness, backaches, varicose veins. I wouldn't want to have to do it.

But if it had been you, I said, and not Rebecca who was pregnant.

Well, I wasn't, was I? And I wasn't the one faced with the decision of having a kid with some loser or having a life. The choice was pretty obvious. I don't blame her. I'd have probably done the same thing.

I looked up at Nathan and he was staring across the backyard with this sad, faraway look on his face, like he was all alone and he probably was. Somewhere out there, I said, there's a woman just waiting for you to come along. Your soul mate.

Naw, he said. That's an old pipe dream I gave up on long ago. You go around thinking that and every day that you don't find her brings misery and self-loathing. No thank you. I'd rather be strung up by my eyelids than subscribe to that way of thinking again.

I stayed with Sal and Kaleigh right through August and into the month of September. Summer heat started to wane and the air grew crisp as lettuce. Jack started school in the fall and boarded a yellow school bus every morning at seven-thirty. We had a regular routine in the store and for the first time in years, maybe in my entire life, I started to understand the benefits of work and stability. My days and nights were easy and I felt peaceful, unruffled by the daily regime of work and sleep. Sometimes, however, I doubted myself. Somewhere in the back of my mind I felt like an impostor, like I wasn't entitled to such good fortune. Sometimes it didn't seem like genuine peace at all but a kind of numbness or forgetting, like skin that is stroked so much it loses all feeling. It was at moments like these that I would disappear downstairs for a session in the tank. I'd let my mind scramble and wear itself out. At first I dreaded ending a float, bursting into the cold basement like a newborn baby, because I always felt raw and slightly vulnerable, like I had to learn to walk all over again, like an amphibian evolving out of water. Gradually though, I drew strength from my meditations. I felt I had a secret life, and like an adulterous husband who returns home with renewed interest in his wife, I emerged seeing the world in a different light.

I became a float tank junkie and Sal was my dealer. I even started to nag him about his idea to start a business. I designed some flyers and came up with a name for the company. THE SALINE SOLUTION. Sal approved, and when he saw how serious I was, let me use his old Mac to print out a few copies to post on the bulletin board in the store. I delivered flyers to all the houses in the area, and we got our first call three days later from a woman by the name of Nora Patson.

Nora was a middle-aged schoolteacher and lived with her older brother who had multiple sclerosis. She figured the tank might be therapeutic for him and a good way to relieve some of the strain on his muscles. Sal was reluctant at first, saying that he had no experience dealing with medical cases and didn't want to be held accountable for any adverse effects. Nora assured him that she would take full responsibility and that, at any rate, her brother would only float under her constant supervision. Sal finally agreed to co-ordinate the sale, called up his supplier in Syracuse and put a down payment of sixteen hundred dollars on a new tank. We drove there early the following Saturday morning, put the two halves of the fibreglass shell into the back of the van, and arrived at Nora's place by one o'clock that afternoon.

It took us four hours to mantle the tank, screw the top on, hook up the motor and install the carbon filters. We laid the blue rubber heating pad on the bottom, then filled the tank using a hose attached to the kitchen sink. We added the Epsom salts, tested the buoyancy of the water and turned on the filtration system. When we were done, Nora gave us tea and cookies and asked if we'd stay until her brother had tried it out. It was kind of exhilarating and pathetic at the same time to watch as she wheeled him out in a pair of baggy pink swimming trunks and lifted him out of his wheelchair. Sal offered to help but she told him that she needed to see if she was capable of doing it on her own. I felt pretty useless listening to her groan under the weight of her brother's twisted limbs while I sipped my tea, but there was nothing to be done. She was used to handling him and her arms were thick and muscular. She managed to get him into the tank and, just before she lowered him into the water, he turned to us and smiled his crooked, blubbering smile. Nora bent into the tank and asked him gently whether he was enjoying the sensation. He must of said yes because she turned and gave us the thumbs up. She wrote out a cheque for the sum of twenty-five hundred dollars and couldn't thank us enough as she walked us to the door.

We were kind of quiet on the drive home.

The next morning, the last Sunday in September, Sal asked me if I wanted to accompany him and Jack to Elroy Deer's annual cider fair. It was an event organized to promote the cider mill and entice new buyers. There was as much free cider as you could drink, a buffet in the evening that his wife and a few of her friends always prepared, a corn-cob roast, then a kind of square dance, hoe-down thing in the evening. It was a cool, windy day and the sky was gunmetal grey as we set off in the van. Elroy's place was a forty-mile drive north-west of Bridgewater, and I passed the time by telling Jack stories about Round Bay and how I used to dive off Adam's Point into the Pacific Ocean. Jack asked me if I'd ever been afraid and I had to think for a moment. I told him that it was partly because I was afraid that I found it so thrilling and that it was because I feared it that I loved it as much as I did. Jack didn't say anything and I figured he didn't really know what I meant. Maybe he did. At any rate, Sal looked over at me and nodded his head like he understood what I was talking about, like I'd just said something wise about the world, something he himself had already figured out.

Eventually, we signalled off the road and turned down a pristine tree-lined avenue and passed under a banner strung up between two poplars, welcoming people to the twenty-third annual cider fair. Stretching out in orderly rows on either side of the white picket fence that marked off the drive were eight square acres of apple trees, their leaves dark red and brown against the bleak sky. We pulled up in front of a freshly painted red farmhouse, surrounded by a clutter of cars and pick-up trucks. Sal parked on the lawn between a brown Volkswagen Rabbit and an old black Saab. We got out and walked around the house, past barrels full of apples, piled high like sweets in front of the barn. I could hear an auctioneer's voice coming over a PA system, taking bids over a background of fiddle music, and the sound of people's voices coming from inside. The barn doors had been propped open by two old tires that were filled with soil and now served as flower pots. A strapping man of middle age, with a white beard, wearing a red cotton shirt and a New York Yankees baseball cap, was standing by the entrance, holding a megaphone and greeting people as they came in.

Salvator Shapiro, he said when he saw us walk in, and he came over and gave Sal a bear hug, practically lifting him off his feet.

Elroy Deer, Sal said. How is it you keep getting better looking every time I see you?

It's Rachel's fault, he said, patting his belly. She's got me on some macrobiotic diet to keep my cholesterol down. And this must be the jackal, he said, picking Jack up effortlessly and perching him on a thick and hairy forearm. You sure have grown, he said in a booming voice, obviously enjoying his role as host, showing off his successful business to anyone who cared to find out just how well he was doing.

Jack smiled and laid his chubby hand on top of Elroy's baseball cap.

Ya, they sure grow fast at his age, Sal said. I'd like you to meet my associate, John Wade. He's been staying with Kaleigh and me since July. We've gone into the flotation business together.

Another entrepreneur, Elroy said, crushing my hand in his firm grip. That's the spirit.

Pleased to meet you, I said, flattered by Sal's introduction. This is quite a place you've got here.

[215]

Yes it is, Elroy said. Quite a handful too. We've been expanding the business, planting more trees, updating the equipment. I'm hiring four more hands in the new year.

Well, there's a market for what you're doing. The health food business is booming, Sal said. I've got a few ideas I'd like to get your opinion on, when you've got a moment.

Well, I'm about ready for a break. Why don't you go inside and get Rachel to give you some of my brandy punch and we'll take a stroll outside?

You mind keeping an eye on Jack for me? Sal asked.

Not at all, I said and took Jack to a table in the corner where they were handing out caramel apples. We sat down on the steps of a makeshift stage where the musicians were set up and ate our treats. When Jack got bored, we went outside into the apple orchard and walked among the trees. We found a stream where we washed our sticky fingers and looked for frogs and tadpoles in the water. We played tag and hide-and-seek until the sun started to go down and a heavy mist was curling round the bottom of the tree trunks. When we got back to the barn, the square dance was underway and I could hear the caller shouting out instructions to bow-to-your-partner, do-si-do. There was a long rectangle of light like a drawbridge outside the barn doors and dust particles floating in the air. We pushed our way through the crowd of sweaty people until I spotted Sal, leaning up against the wall chatting to a young woman with cropped hair and wearing a pale blue business outfit. Every time he threw his head back to laugh, his glasses caught the light and flashed white. When he saw us coming, he pushed himself off the wall and came forward.

Hey John, he said. Want you to meet Cindy. She's an A&P representative. They're thinking of buying shares in Elroy's cider business. It'll mean big money for him in the future.

Sure, I said, looking at Cindy's heavily made-up face.

It's my first big assignment as Assistant Director of Sales, she said, taking a sip of her punch, leaving a red stain on the Styrofoam cup.

That's great, I said.

It's a pretty stressful job, she said. But I belong to a gym and do aerobics three times a week. It's a really good release of tension.

You hungry? Sal asked, squatting down and addressing his son. Can you get him something to eat? he said, looking up at me.

Come on, Jack, I said. Let's go.

Jack and I left the din of the barnyard behind and found a small pocket of people standing around a table behind the house. They were smoking cigarettes and warming their hands over a kerosene stove. A woman was handing out corn-cobs with a large metal fork. We sat down side by side on an empty picnic table and ate our corn and I pretended to be a typewriter, biting my way across the cob, chomp-chomp-chomp-ding, and back to the other end. Jack laughed and tried it himself, over and over again until he was finished. Then he snuggled up on my lap and I stroked his head until he had fallen asleep. When I was certain he wouldn't wake, I carried him over to the van and laid him across the back seat. I took Sal's jacket and tucked it in around his little body. I kissed him on the forehead and wandered back into the barn. Sal was exactly where we'd left him, still talking to that A&P rep. He was telling her something that was making her smile. His mouth was very close to her ear and his hand was travelling down the small of her back when I interrupted them.

Whaddya want? he asked and I could smell alcohol on his breath. His face was flushed and his rosy cheeks were like two polished apples.

Jack's asleep, I said.

Good for him, he said.

Don't you think we should be heading off?

Sal straightened up and Cindy looked down at her patent leather shoes. Maybe next time, she said and one after the other adjusted the lapels of her blazer and smoothed the material across her collar bone.

Sal sighed, took off his glasses and rubbed his face.

See ya round, she said and wandered off.

Sal glared at me with unfocussed eyes. You're a real killjoy, you know that? he said as we left the barn and headed over to the van.

You'll thank me tomorrow, I said.

I will not.

I thought you didn't drink.

I don't, he said and fumbled with his keys.

I'll drive, I said.

Fuck off, he said and pushed me sideways.

Think about Jack, I said, and he sobered up for a moment and handed me the keys.

The drive home was dark and quiet. Sal fell asleep in the front seat and I listened to his laboured breathing overlap with his son's quick breath and thought about my own father. I remembered how he'd come into my room one night smelling of booze and sat down on the edge of my bed. I was afraid of him and pretended to be asleep. After a while, he pulled the covers up and tucked them under my chin. He even stroked my head before leaving the room and I lay awake for a long time wondering what he'd been thinking. When we got back to the Emporium, I shook Sal awake. Here, I said and handed him a piece of gum.

Thanks, he said and ran a hand through his thick hair. He carried Jack into the house and I flopped down onto the sofa. Kaleigh came out to the back porch in her dressing gown and sat down on the arm.

I made you a bed in Jack's room, she said. I thought, now that summer's over, it might be getting a bit cold out here. I know he won't mind. It'll be like a sleep-over for him.

Are you sure? I asked.

Ya, she said. Come on up.

I followed the fresh, clean smell of her shampoo up the stairs, watching the outline of her hips move under her gown. She showed me into Jack's room and pointed to a mattress on the floor.

I hope you'll be comfortable, she said.

I'm sure I will be, I said, watching her pull the covers up under Jack's chin. She kneeled down and fluffed up my pillow. She pulled the blanket back and folded it over neatly. There, she said and stood up. Goodnight, sweetie, she said and gave me a kiss on the cheek. Sleep well. See you in the morning.

I got undressed and located the bed on the floor. I turned out the light and dove onto the mattress. I lay on my back and pulled the fresh covers up to my chest. I looked up and the ceiling was flecked with glow-in-the-dark stars. It was like sleeping outdoors, made the room feel infinitely big. I thought about the kind of childhood Jack was having, about the kind of father Sal was, and couldn't be angry with him anymore. All the flirting in the world didn't amount to much when you compared it to the love of a good father.

As I was dropping off to sleep, I heard the bed next door begin to creak, slowly at first, then gradually the noise became frantic. I lay stock still and listened as their breathing grew fast and urgent. I heard a muffled grunt and Kaleigh moaned. Someone sighed and the house relapsed into silence.

By the third week in October, the Saline Solution had transacted three more sales and taken in a profit of eight hundred and fifty dollars. Because Sal thought I'd done most of the work of promoting the business, he let me keep half the money. I borrowed the van and drove into town and opened up a bank account. I bought myself another pair of jeans and a second-hand winter jacket. On the way back, I stopped off at the market and bought a pumpkin.

It was late afternoon and it had begun to rain. I watched the tree trunks slowly change from grey to black as the water leaked down through the branches. As I was getting out of the van, Jack's school bus stopped at the curb. The door folded open with a sigh and Jack hopped down. He came running towards me in that side-to-side way, his huge knapsack always a second behind, bouncing left as he put his right foot down, always swinging at counter-purposes.

I turned and lifted the pumpkin out of the van. Look what I

bought for you, I said and bumped him backwards with the smooth round side of the pumpkin.

Are you gonna carve it? he asked.

Yep, I said. But I need your help.

When Kaleigh saw me coming through the store with a pumpkin in my arms, she frowned and said, I was going to get one of those tomorrow.

Well, I saved you the trip. This was the best one they had, I said, putting it down on the counter.

You got another call from a woman about a tank, she said. I left the message by the phone. New jacket?

Army Surplus special, I said.

Looks warm.

It is, I said. I'm sweating to death.

Well, you'll need it when the winter comes.

Kaleigh looked at Jack and smoothed his hair. Any homework to do?

Nope, he said.

You sure?

Can we carve the pumpkin?

I guess that's up to John.

Sure, I said. We'll need one of your felt pens to draw the face.

I'll go get one, Jack said and ran upstairs. I followed him up and put the pumpkin on the kitchen table. I took my jacket off, went into the hall and over to the phone. A Miss Avery had called and left her number. I dialled and a woman answered in a husky voice.

Hi, I said. My name's John. I'm calling from the Saline Solution.

Oh yes, she said. I was hoping to talk to Sal.

He's busy at the moment, but I can get him to call you later.

Well, I'll probably see him soon, she said and paused.

So, um, you're interested in buying a tank? I asked.

Well, I was kind of hoping for a trial run.

We can arrange that, I said. We've got one here and you're welcome to use it. The water's continually being filtered, so it's perfectly hygienic.

Well, maybe you can just get Sal to give me a call when he's got the chance.

Sure, I said. If you want.

Ya, that would be great, she said. Thanks a lot.

No problem, I said, hung up the phone and went back into the kitchen. Jack came in and handed me a blue felt pen. I took some newspaper out of the recycling bin on the floor and spread it over the table. What do you want it to look like? I asked, taking a knife out of the drawer.

Scary, Jack said. With fangs and scary eyes.

Okay, I said and drew a mouth with jagged teeth. I drew two slits for eyes and two eyebrows that came down in a sharp point in the middle. I picked up the knife and made the first incision. The blade resisted, bending slightly against the hard shell, then punctured the thick skin and plunged deep into the soft, fleshy centre.

It was Monday, October 31st, Halloween morning and two days before my nineteenth birthday. Sal had arranged for Miss Avery to come by and have a float at ten o'clock in the morning, so after breakfast I went down to the basement and cleaned the tank. I placed a fresh towel on the card table and rewound the tape. Kaleigh had given me a can of ozone-friendly air freshener because she said the basement always smelt damp and mildewy to her. I sprayed the air a few times then went back upstairs. It's all ready, I told Sal, and he looked up briefly over his cup of coffee.

I was standing at the checkout counter, covering for Kaleigh who was on her break, when Miss Avery walked in. She was wearing a long, camel hair coat and flat leather shoes. Her hair was tucked up under a black beret and her face was free of make-up. She was carrying a brown leather shoulder bag and when she came over I could smell her perfume.

Hi, she said, extending her hand.

Hi, I answered, aware of the soft, dry skin of her hand in mine.

I recognize your voice, she said. I spoke with you on the phone.

You must be Miss Avery.

That's right, she said. Sal around?

He's in the storeroom, I said. I'll go get him.

Sal was washing his hands at the sink when I walked in. She's here, I said and he looked up.

What was that? he asked.

Miss Avery.

Oh, right, he said and smoothed his hair before leaving the room. Miss Avery, he said in a singsong voice. It's good to see you again, and he took her soft, dry hand in his.

Sal led her downstairs and I felt my heart drop into my stomach. I don't know why, it just did. I could hear their muffled voices under the floorboards and her throaty laugh. I sat down on a stool by the cash register and slowly unwrapped a date square, trying not to tear the Saran-Wrap. As I was pressing the last crumbs of oatmeal onto the pads of my fingertips, I started to feel nervous, like there was a strange presence in the room and then I realized that it was silence. I couldn't hear their voices anymore. I longed for a customer to walk in, anything to occupy my mind. I stood up and walked over to the front door and looked outside. I heard Kaleigh move around upstairs and started to panic. I didn't want her to come downstairs. I glanced at the door to the basement and then at the clock on the wall. She had another five minutes left on her break. I walked to the opposite end of the store and paused in front of the basement door. I thought of knocking, tightening my hand around the doorknob and twisting it. I stared at the PRIVATE sign like it was a blatant lie. There was nothing private about it. Not in his own house, under the same roof. It wasn't right. I stood there chewing my lip and rubbing my hands together. I felt torn. I looked over my shoulder towards the stairs then back again. I was just about to reach for the handle when the door opened and Sal walked out, soft music floating out behind him. He stopped and looked at me, then quietly pulled the door shut.

What? he asked.

I thought I noticed a little moisture on his upper lip.

What are you looking at me like that for? he said.

I shook my head. Nothing, I said.

You know you can talk to me if something's wrong, he said.

I nodded my head.

Okay, well I'll be in the storeroom if you need me. And nobody goes downstairs for the next hour, got that?

I nodded again.

That evening I sat in the kitchen while Kaleigh put the finishing touches on Jack's Halloween costume. He was going as a pumpkin and she was sewing a bright orange pillowcase onto an orange turtleneck that she'd bought that week.

I hope I can get these stitches out without ruining the turtleneck, she said. Jack looks so cute in it. It was a great idea, John, the ignis fatuus.

The what?

Well, I didn't know either until I looked it up. It's the original concept behind the Jack-o'-lantern, she said, laying her needle down and looking at me. Ignis fatuus, will-o'-the-wisp, Jack-o'-lantern, they're all the same thing.

What does it mean? I asked.

They're symbols of deception. Apparently there's a kind of phosphorescence that's generated over marshes, anywhere where there's a lot of vegetable decay. It's from the gases that are released and it glows in the dark. Story has it that people would follow the light thinking that it was a spirit or a ghost and more often than not it led them straight into a marsh or a bog where they would drown. It's a symbol of delusion, of being led by false hope. In Russian folklore, this light represents the spirits of stillborn children wandering the earth between heaven and the Inferno.

Kaleigh waited for my reaction. I raised my eyebrows and nodded slowly. So we aren't to follow any pumpkins tonight, I said.

That's right, she answered, smiling at me and sticking her needle back into the material and pulling it out. Except for Jack, she said. You stick to him like glue. I have mixed feelings about Halloween. I know it's only superstition, but it kind of gives me the creeps. I'm not crazy about it, she said, pulling the thread and snapping it off with her strong white teeth. You gonna be okay with Jack?

Oh yeah, I said. No problem.

I had offered to take Jack trick-or-treating because Mary-Beth had put her back out and been in bed all week and Kaleigh wanted to take her some food and spend the evening over there.

He's pretty excited, she said. I think what you've got with Jack is really sweet. He absolutely adores you. I wonder what's gonna happen?

Whaddya mean?

When you leave. I mean, I can't imagine you wanting to stay here forever.

I kind of like it here, I said.

Well, she said, we like having you too. It's good for Sal. He enjoys the extra company. I know I can't be everything to him and sometimes I feel we're too isolated out here. Not enough stimulation, you know? There, she said, holding up the pumpkin top and turning it around. She'd cut a mouth and eyes out of black felt and glued them to the front. All I've got to do now is stuff these pillows in and we're set.

Kaleigh called Jack and he came into the kitchen, wearing orange tights and orange shorts so that he looked like he'd been dipped up to the waist in paint. Kaleigh pulled the turtleneck carefully over his head and fluffed up the pillows. She pulled a green balaclava over his head for the stem and smiled. You look so cute, she said, squeezing his arms, I could eat you up. Where's your daddy?

He's in the shower, Jack said.

Well, tell him I've gone to Mary-Beth's and won't be back till late. Now you behave yourself tonight and do as John tells you. Have a wonderful time, she said and started putting the soup and bread and the Nanaimo bars she'd baked into a shallow cardboard box. She gave Jack a kiss and pulled on her coat.

I'll carry that, I said, picking up the box and following her downstairs.

Kaleigh? I said. I just wanted to say thanks for everything, you know. You guys have been really good to me.

Aw, sweetie, she said, raising her hand and stroking my cheek. It's nothing, really. You've always pulled your weight around here. It hasn't been hard having you around.

I walked her out to the van, went around the other side and placed the box on the passenger seat. Watch out for goblins, she said, giving me a wink and starting the engine.

I watched her back down the drive and reverse into the road. I walked to the front of the house and watched the van disappear around the bend. The air was damp and a cold wind was picking up. There were pumpkins on every porch in the neighbourhood, candlelight trembling in their mouths and eye sockets. Across the street, next to the curb, a mail box had been transformed into a ghost and the pale blue sheet flapped in the breeze. I heard children's voices and a gang of American presidents came walking down the road. One of them raised a hand and waved at me. I thought I recognized Maude's girlish figure and waved back. I felt a raindrop land on my face and looked up. The sky was a nuclear orange. I lifted the lid of our own pumpkin and pulled the candle out

of the hole I'd dug with a spoon. I took a pack of matches out
of my pocket, cupped my hand around the wick and lit it. I
twisted it back into the spongy flesh, replaced the lid and
stepped back. The pumpkin flickered to life. It grinned at me,
a knowing grin, as if it was wise to something I couldn't see,
as if it was laughing at me. I turned and headed back into the
house.

When I got to the kitchen, Jack jumped up and said, Can
we go now? It's already dark.

Sure, I said. Just let me get my coat.

I walked down the hall towards the bedroom. Sal was still
in the bathroom and I could hear him humming softly to
himself. I knocked on the door and he opened it a crack. Yes?
he said and I could smell his aftershave like a guilty conscience.

I'm taking Jack out now.

Take your time, he said. When d'ya think you'll be back?

I dunno, I said.

About an hour?

I guess, I said. Why?

I've got some work to do and I'd appreciate the peace and
quiet.

Sure, I said. See ya later.

I took Jack's hand and we left the house, that all-seeing,
lunatic pumpkin at our backs, laughing us to the curb, mocking our good intentions and our naïve faith in the world, as if
to say tonight of all nights was beyond our control. I
squeezed Jack's hand a little tighter then while the wind
blew across our faces, making Jack's plastic bag rattle like lit-
ter blown through an empty street. We crossed the street to

the house where Elizabeth lived, an elderly widow with a wizened apple-doll face. Jack rang the bell and the door opened.

Trick-or-treat, Jack sung out, holding his A&P bag open with both hands.

Well, hello there, she said. And who might you be?

I'm Jack-o'-lantern, he said proudly.

What a wonderful costume, she said. I didn't recognize you at first. Here you go, and she dropped a handful of brightly wrapped suckers into the bag. Here's one for you, John, she said and plucked one from the bowl and handed it to me like a short stemmed rose.

Thanks Liz, I said and led Jack across her lawn to the house next door. While we were waiting for the door to open, I looked over my shoulder and saw a car slow down in front of the Appleseed Emporium, its headlights fanning out in an arc as it turned into the drive. I watched a woman get out in a long beige coat. I recognized the coat and the black beret and slowly turned back again. I put my hand on Jack's shoulder as he held his bag open for another handful of candy. I wanted to protect him, to take him away and prevent his world from caving in. I wanted to preserve his innocence even when I knew that it was impossible. Everything around me, the electricity in the air, the distant shouts and screams as children scurried between the houses, all of it seemed menacing. I held Jack's small hand firmly in mine as if he might be wrenched from me at any moment. I felt another raindrop land on my face and looked up. The sky was the colour of a yellow bruise. Another drop fell on my face. Shit, I said, it's raining.

I don't wanna go home! Jack cried.

We won't go back, I said. Not now. Not yet.

When we finally got back to the house, we were soaked right through. My head was cold and rain was dripping off the end of my nose like it was a goddamn faucet. Jack's costume was sagging and his tights were all bunched up around his ankles. He was clutching his loot bag and shivering. When we got to the front door, I pulled the balaclava off his head and could see by the front light that his lips were blue. Miss Avery's car was still parked outside, so I rang the doorbell. Nobody answered and Jack looked up at me still shaking with cold. I rang the doorbell again and tried the door. It was unlocked and we rushed in stamping our feet and shaking the rain out of our hair.

Sal came down the stairs two at a time. Why didn't you come in round the back? he said.

I thought you might be busy, I said, anger rising up in me at the sight of his dry crumpled clothes and flushed cheeks. I noticed that the bowl of caramelized popcorn that Kaleigh had prepared and left by the door was still full to the brim.

Not at all, he said. Just meeting with a client. We're finalizing a sale, he said, helping Jack step out of his shoes. You're freezing, he said, rubbing his arms up and down.

Look at all my candy, Jack said, his teeth chattering like bone dice.

Good God, Sal said. You're not going to eat all that crap, are you?

Yes, he answered.

We'll see about that, Sal said, pulling the pumpkin pillows

over Jack's head. Go run a bath, he said, peeling off his shorts and tights. Jack had bright pink patches on his thighs and his hands and toes were rosy red. Sal patted him on the bum and he took off upstairs. He squealed as he passed Miss Avery on the stairs.

I should really be going now, Miss Avery said, floating elegantly across the floor.

I'll call you when the tank is ready for delivery, I heard Sal say as I headed up the stairs. I got undressed and crawled into bed. I could hear Jack splashing around in the bathtub, talking to himself. I pulled the blankets up over my head and curled into a tight ball like a fist ready for the punch.

Kaleigh woke me up with a cup of tea the next morning.

Jack's not going to school, she said. He's got a cold. How are you feeling this morning?

Not so good, I said. I'm all plugged up.

What were you thinking last night? she asked. Sal said Jack's lips were all blue when he got home. Why didn't you come back for an umbrella at least?

I didn't want to disappoint him, I said.

He's just a kid, she said in a desperate voice. Sometimes you have to lay down the rules. It's for his own good.

I looked over at Jack asleep in his bed. He didn't want to stop, I said.

Of course he didn't, she said. But you were supposed to be looking after him.

I thought I was.

Well, think again, she said and got up and went over to Jack's bed. She caressed his head, then tucked the covers in all around his body, down his legs and under his feet. She gave him a kiss and left the room.

Later that afternoon, I heard Sal and Kaleigh having an argument. It was the first time I'd ever heard them raise their voices at each other. Kaleigh yelled something about how Sal was always so busy that he never spent any time with Jack, and Sal yelled back something about how reckless I had been and that maybe it wasn't healthy the way Jack was so attached to me. He just didn't like it, he said. Then Kaleigh asked him what it was that he had to do that was so important last night he couldn't even take his own son trick-or-treating.

Jack leaned up in bed and sneezed. He wiped his nose with the back of his hand and said, Happy Birthday, John.

I looked up at his puffy face and felt my heart rip open inside my chest. I blinked and lay down again. Go to sleep, Jack. My birthday's not until tomorrow.

I woke again in darkness. The sun had gone down and I didn't know what time it was. I looked over at Jack's bed and it was empty. I sat up and rubbed my throat. The house was quiet and I could hear the murmur of voices in another room. I got up and pulled my jeans on. I put on my sweatshirt and opened the door and walked down the hall to the kitchen. Kaleigh was sitting with Jack on her lap, rocking him gently back and forth. Sal was making a cup of coffee. He turned to look at me.

Feeling any better? Kaleigh asked.

A bit, I said, standing awkwardly in the doorway.

We want you to get better for the big party tomorrow night.

What party? I asked.

Your birthday dinner, Sal said.

You didn't think we'd forget, she said.

How could we? Sal said. With Jack reminding us every five minutes.

Well, it's not a big deal, I said, torn between gratitude and resentment. You don't need to make a fuss.

You look pale, Kaleigh said quietly.

I'm still not feeling very well, I said.

Then why don't you go back to bed? Sal suggested.

What time is it?

Nine o'clock, he said, glaring at me. I backed out of the kitchen and walked slowly towards the bedroom. I sat down on Jack's bed and put my head in my hands. Maybe I'd out-stayed my welcome. Maybe I wasn't wanted anymore. Maybe my presence was putting a strain on their relation-ship. Whatever the case, whatever the consequence, I wasn't quite ready to give it all up. I had finally found somewhere to belong and I clung to that feeling like a prisoner's final hope of escape. I tried to convince myself that everything would turn out alright, but as I tried to fall asleep again I imagined I could hear a tiny noise, the ominous sound of a chisel on stone, as if someone was in the basement chipping away at the foundation, as if, once again, my world had inevitably started to crumble.

I felt better in the morning. I got up early and went into the kitchen to make myself a cup of coffee. Sal was sitting read-ing the newspaper. He looked up when I came in and smiled.

Nate's coming round first thing this morning, he said. He's got something for you.

[233]

Really? I asked. It was Wednesday morning, the second of November and I was now officially nineteen years old. Maybe we could make a fresh start of it after all.

So how does it feel to be nineteen?

I dunno. Ask me in a year from now.

Listen, John, could you do me a favour?

What?

I was supposed to go get some stuff in Albany today, but things are a bit hectic in the store. I've got some paperwork to do, you know, and I'm way behind on the books, so I was wondering if you could go pick it up.

Sure, I said. You should really stay and tend to things here.

What's that supposed to mean? he asked.

Never mind, I said and suddenly I couldn't see the old Sal anymore. I no longer saw the father figure I'd looked up to or the man who'd taken me in and befriended me.

Why are you looking at me like that? he said, holding the paper down on his lap.

I don't know, I said.

Look, John. People in glass houses shouldn't throw stones.

What the fuck is that supposed to mean?

I just don't want you to do anything you'll regret.

Likewise, I said.

It's none of your business.

Then what about Kaleigh?

I don't think you should talk about things you know nothing about, Sal said, shaking his paper out and raising it in front of his face.

Morning fellas, Kaleigh said, coming into the kitchen in her dressing gown and slippers.

I'm going downstairs, I said.

How are you feeling today? she asked.

Better, thanks, I said, and shot Sal a look before leaving the room.

As I was going down the stairs, I heard someone open the back door and come into the store. I heard Nathan call out a greeting and went over to meet him.

It's the birthday boy, he said, slapping me on the shoulder. N-n-n-n-nineteen.

Ya, ya, so what, I said.

Don't tell me, birthdays depress you. It's a nationwide affliction. You just have to learn to accept the passage of time.

Sometimes I wish it would go faster.

Now, now. Can't be that bad. Trouble in paradise?

You could say that again, I said.

Trouble in paradise.

I'm being serious, Nathan.

Come on, he said gently. I've got something that'll cheer you up.

What? I asked him.

Right this way, he said, and I followed him outside. As we rounded the house he said, Remember that old write-off you brought me three months ago? Bet you thought I'd forgotten about it. Well, I took it under my wing and voilà. Runs like a dream now, so she does.

There it was, my little Dodge Omni, polished and buffed to a brilliant, waxy finish, sparkling in the sour autumn sunshine. I can't believe it, I whispered, feeling like I'd just been given a gift I didn't quite deserve.

New timing belt, water pump, spark plugs. Battery's been

charged up and she's ready to roll, Nathan said, clasping his hands behind his back and raising himself onto the balls of his feet with the air of a surgeon who'd just given a patient a second chance at life.

Aw, Nate, I said. You're a fucken star. I can't believe it. How much do I owe you?

Nothing, he said. Sal gave me some money from your earnings to cover the parts and I enjoyed doing the work.

I don't know what to say, I said.

Don't worry about it, kid, and he handed me the keys.

This is the best birthday present I've ever got in my whole entire life, I said and opened the door and got in. I sat behind the wheel and ran my hands around the moulded plastic. I inserted the key and started the engine. I revved it a little then turned it off.

Sounds good, I said, getting out.

Well, I didn't need you to tell me that.

I know, I said and smiled. Do you wanna coffee or somethin'?

Sure, he said. Are the Flintstones up yet?

Ya, they're in the kitchen, I said and followed him back into the house.

Jack was up and eating a bowl of cornflakes, which was as close to eating junk food as Kaleigh would allow. Kaleigh was making some tea and Sal was still reading the paper. So, he said as I walked in. Get your surprise?

Ya, I'm really pleased, I said, tempering my enthusiasm.

You want some breakfast, Nate? Kaleigh asked, looking over her shoulder.

Thanks, sweetheart, he answered and tousled Jack's hair.

So you gonna go to Albany? Sal asked me again.

What for? Kaleigh said.

Those new vitamin supplements.

Oh.

I can take my car, I said.

Is he gonna have enough room, Sal? Shouldn't he take the van?

It's just a couple of boxes, baby, he said. I'll go get the receipts.

Sal left the kitchen and returned a few minutes later with some forms and a road map of Albany. He opened it up on the kitchen table and circled a street on the outskirts of town.

You shouldn't have a problem finding the place. Give me a call if they give you any trouble.

I'll leave now, I said, folding the map and tucking it into my back pocket.

Great, Sal said. Make a day of it.

I will.

Don't forget, John. We're gonna have a little bash this evening, Kaleigh said. Can you be home by six? I don't want it to be too late 'cause Jack's got school tomorrow.

Sure, I said and touched Nathan's arm on the way out. Thanks again, I said and walked down the hall. I got my jacket and went downstairs. I got into the car and sat for a while before inserting the key. It felt strange to be back in my Omni, as if the last three months had been some sort of a dream and I was right back where I began. I started the engine and reversed out the drive. I rolled my window down although it was cool. Dark clouds were gathering to the east in the direction I was headed. I switched the radio on and cranked it up. It was good to be going somewhere again, good to feel the rotation of the tires beneath me and the freedom of the endless miles ahead.

I stopped at a gas station on the highway and filled the tank, bought a Coke and a sandwich and lingered at the counter for a while, then asked for a pack of cigarettes. I got back into the car, tapped a cigarette onto the back of my hand and lit up. I inhaled the thick hot smoke and felt the nicotine seeping through my veins, relaxing all my limbs. I'd missed the crazy comfort that tobacco brings, like an old friend, the reassurance that everything is gonna be okay. I finished that one and lit another. I started the car and drove on until the sign for a liquor store caught my eye. Before I had a chance to think about it, I had pulled over and gotten out. I bought a bottle of good old-fashioned Jack Daniels, which I tucked into the pocket of my army surplus jacket, and got back into the car. I sat by the side of the road and ate my sandwich. The sky was now entirely grey. I took a swig of JD and it started to rain.

When I got to Albany, I didn't even bother picking up Sal's order. I went straight to a bar and sat down. The barmaid came over and put a napkin down in front of me.

What can I get for you? she asked.

Can I have a Bud please?

Can I have some ID please?

I left my wallet at home, I said.

So how you gonna pay for this?

I've got some money, I said and took my wallet out of my

pocket and, holding it in my lap, pulled out all the money I had and placed it on the bar.

You gonna drink all that? she asked.

Yep, I nodded.

Then I suggest you go for something a little bit more expensive.

Anything'll do.

I'll get you a whiskey, she said and walked down the bar. She came back and placed a drink on the napkin in front of me and said, Just for the record, I know you're under age. But seeing as we're not really doing any business right now, I'll let you stay.

Thanks, I said. I appreciate it. I'm having a bit of a bad day.

Ya, well, getting drunk's not gonna change that.

I know, but it helps.

Sure, she said. Temporarily. But at the end of the day, you still gotta go home and face whatever it is that you're avoiding.

Home? I said. I don't even know what that means anymore.

Home is where your best memories reside.

Well, then I've lost it. I lost it a long time ago.

So what are you running away from then?

I dunno, I said. Myself.

Rain was coming down in sheets and it was seven-thirty by the time I got back to the health food store. I was drunk and nearly back-ended the van parked in the driveway. I tripped on the porch steps and banged my head on the screen door. I staggered through the store, up the stairs and into the kitchen. Kaleigh and Nathan were sitting at the table around the

[239]

remains of what was supposed to have been my birthday supper. I could smell pot in the air and Kaleigh's eyes were red and her lids looked heavy.

I was sure that you were gone, she said when she saw me come in.

Where the fuck have you been? Nathan said. Jack's all upset. He made you a cake and everything.

I'm sorry, I said, swaying slightly.

You smell like a brewery, he said.

I pulled what was left of the JD from my coat pocket and placed the bottle on the table and sat down.

Well, at least the boy's got taste, Nathan said and poured himself a shot.

Nate, Kaleigh said. Please put that away before Sal gets back. You know how he gets.

Where's the boss? I asked.

He's having a float, she said. He seemed pretty stressed out today.

I'm sure he was, I said.

What's that supposed to mean? Nathan asked.

Never mind, I answered and felt a little hand tug at my sleeve. I turned to see Jack's sweet, innocent face and bent down to give him a hug. He squirmed out of my arms and said, You stink.

I've been drinking, I said.

How come? Jack asked me.

'Cause I felt like it.

You've been smoking too, Kaleigh said, waving a hand in front of her nose. Come on, Jack, say goodnight. You're supposed to be in bed.

But my bedtime's not until eight o'clock.

I don't want to hear about it! she snapped.

I'm not going.

Now! she said in such a sharp voice that even she seemed to be surprised by the sound of it. Jack looked up at her and started to cry.

But I want John to read me a story, he whined.

Not tonight, she said.

Why not?

Because I'm your mom and I'm telling you, no!

I don't wanna go to bed! he screamed.

How 'bout I read you a story, Nathan suggested, standing up and going over to Jack and picking him up.

Let me down! he cried, thrashing about in his arms.

Jack, you go with Nate right this minute or mommy's gonna spank you!

Everybody in the room turned to look at Kaleigh. Jack had never been spanked before in his life, not that I knew of, and he stopped kicking and let Nathan hold him.

I wanna say goodnight to John, he sniffled, so Nathan put him down and he came over to me. He looked at me very seriously and put a hand on my leg. I made you a cake, he said and it broke my heart. Daddy said you weren't coming back but I didn't believe him.

Jack walked over to the fridge and pulled the door open. See? he said and I got up slowly and walked over. On the top shelf was a square chocolate cake with the words *Happy B-day John* written in blue icing.

It's beautiful, I said.

Come on, Jack, Nathan said. It's time for bed. I'll read you anything you want. Jack felt for my hand and looked up at me. I smiled feebly and nodded for him to go. He gave his mom a kiss and waddled like a duck out of the kitchen in his blue pajamas with the yellow feet. Nathan glanced back at us, then disappeared down the hall.

I sat down and poured myself another drink. I reached inside my jacket and pulled out my cigarettes. I put one in my mouth and offered the pack to Kaleigh.

Why not, she said, and took one too. I held the lighter up for her and she took a drag and coughed. It's been a while.

Who cares? I said.

I'm just saying, she said.

Guess you don't have room in your perfect little life for a vice like smoking.

Don't be nasty, John.

I'm sorry, I said. I'm not mad at you.

Well who the hell are you so mad at then?

Your husband.

My husband has a name.

Sal, I said. He's a fucken hypocrite. He's got this squeaky-clean image that he holds over everyone, but it's all a front. He's not like that, you know.

I know he's not perfect.

You don't know anything about him.

Oh, for chrissake, John. I've been with the man for eight years, she said, stubbing her cigarette out on a plate and taking a sip of water.

And does he make you happy? I asked.

Kaleigh paused. Well, for your information, yes he does, she said. Most of the time. Look, you shouldn't take it personally if he loses his patience or is hard to work with. He gets moody sometimes, but it's no big deal.

It's not that, I said.

Everybody slips up from time to time.

I just want to know if he makes you happy, that's all.

I already told you that he does, she said, raising her voice.

Well, I don't think he deserves you.

It's not a question of deserving. If it was, nobody would ever get together. People aren't perfect. Most of them aren't even that nice to begin with.

I just can't stand the way he lies to you. Right to your face, and you keep going along with it, making dinner, cleaning up, practically his servant. Someone ought to make him face up and take responsibility.

Like you? she sneered.

He gets away with murder.

What are you talking about? she said.

I'm talking about Miss Avery, I blurted out.

She's a client.

She's a fuck of a lot more than that, I said, lighting another cigarette off the one I'd just finished.

I really wish you wouldn't smoke in the house.

Get real, Kaleigh. That's the least of your worries.

Oh, really?

Ya. Your husband is running around screwing God knows how many women, right under your nose, and all you can do is worry about a little bit of cigarette smoke.

Fuck you, she said.

It's true, Kaleigh. I saw him.

I can't believe you're telling me this.

It's for your own good, I said.

You know what, John? You're an arrogant, supercilious little son of a bitch. What have you got to loose, huh? You feel indignant at the injustices of the world? Feel you have the right to go on a moral rampage? Well, how the fuck do you think I feel? I've put eight years of my life into this relationship and you, you feel justified in criticizing me?

I'm not criticizing you, I said.

You come breezing in off the street, see a flaw in my marriage and tear the whole thing to shreds. Is that what you do? What are you? The morality police? Well, go ahead. See what I care. I'm not gonna flinch just because you feel like being a bully. I've got a kid and a husband and a house and a business to loose in the bargain. You're just a little hobo. You're not committed to anything. You can come and go whenever you goddamn please and it wouldn't make a blind bit of difference to you. Well, I can't, she said, seething, the words shooting out between her teeth, her face red and blotchy. Her eyes were moist and suddenly tears came pouring out, streaming down her cheeks. She got up and went over to the sink.

I just hate to see Sal doing this to you, I said. I care about you. I care about Jack. I don't think you should have to put up with this. I think you should leave him.

I can't just get up and go, she said, turning around. I'm stuck here, don't you understand that? I can't just take Jack and leave. How would I survive, huh? How would I get by? Besides, Sal's done more for me than anybody could ever dream of, and you know what? I don't give a fuck whether or not he screws some little tart if it makes him happy. I make the best of our life. You think I'm deluded? Need to be set straight? Well, I think you're the one who's deluded. Do you have any idea what it takes to make a relationship last? It's not magic. Or romance, either. It's a fuck of a lot of hard work and compromise. I have to make an effort and so does Sal. Which is probably a concept that has never even occurred to you. Something you've probably never had to do in your whole life. You've probably never risked your precious little ego by sticking your neck out for anyone. You've probably never forgiven anybody in your entire life. Never had to, because you have no attachments. You just leave, don't you, she said, accusing me with her eyes.

You think there's such a thing as true love? she went on. The perfect nuclear family? Well, that's a textbook dream of the fifties, concocted by men who'd just come back from a war and wanted more than anything else in the world to be lulled to sleep at night by their mothers. It's not a reality for real people. Real people are fucked up. Do you understand what I'm saying? They're lonely and they're weak and they're selfish and nothing in your life is ever gonna turn out the way you expect it to. Do you hear me? she said, wiping her face with the back of her hand and turning away. You're so young, she said. You're so fucken naïve.

Kaleigh stood at the sink staring at her reflection in the window, raindrops like necklaces of silver beads sliding down the pane. The house was quiet. I stared at the burning end of my cigarette, unable to smoke or move. I felt as cold and hard as a diamond. I heard someone coming up the stairs and Sal walked in wearing flip-flops and a pair of baggy jogging pants. He had a towel slung over his shoulder.

[245]

What's up? he asked and Kaleigh shook her head. Sal peered down the hallway and ducked back out. I heard voices whispering in the hall and started to feel afraid.

Sal and Nathan came back into the kitchen and Sal looked down at the cigarette butts and the near-empty bottle of Jack Daniels on the table. What's going on? he said and stroked Kaleigh's head. He pulled the hair back that had fallen forward over her face and tucked it behind her ear. What's the matter, sweetheart?

Nothing, she said, shaking her head and hiding behind her hair again.

I really should be going, Nathan said.

No, no. I want you to stay, Sal said.

No, I don't think that's a good idea. You wanna come back with me tonight, John?

No way, Sal said. I wanna get to the bottom of this. I think we need to have a little chat.

Oh, shut up, Kaleigh said. You're so trite about everything.

What, me? he asked, pointing at his chest. What have I done now?

Kaleigh glared at him and the blood drained out of her face. I know, she said slowly, almost inaudibly, about you and Miss Avery. John told me.

Sal clenched his jaw. A vein bulged at his temple. He's lying, he said. He doesn't know what he's talking about.

It doesn't take a genius, Sal.

Look, he thinks he saw something, but he didn't, okay?

Why should I believe you? she said, sighing heavily.

I don't think I want to have this discussion right now, Sal said.

[246]

You mean, *again*. You don't want to have this discussion *again*.

No, not now, not ever, he said. You know, you should really get your facts straight before you go around accusing people of things they didn't do. It's all lies, Kaleigh. But you go ahead and believe them if you want to. You must really love me to believe them in the first place.

Don't you dare, she said. Don't you dare turn this around on me.

And why not? How do you think this makes me feel, huh?

You? she yelled. You? How do I think this makes *you* feel?

Ya, he said.

Kaleigh shook her head. She brought her hands up and covered her face. I can't believe this, she whispered. Oh Christ, tell me this isn't happening again. I can't deal with this. I really can't.

Kaleigh? Sal said, touching her arm.

Forget it, she said. Just forget it. I'm going to go to bed now. Please, she said, pulling her arm away. Just leave me alone.

Kaleigh crossed the room. She looked at Nathan on her way out and he dropped his eyes. I could hear her go into the bathroom and shut the door. She turned on the faucet and I glanced over at Sal. He sat down at the table and put his head in his hands. The door to the bathroom opened and he looked up. Another door closed as Kaleigh went into the bedroom. Sal reached over and wrapped his fingers around my bottle of JD.

Don't, Nathan said, putting his hand on Sal's shoulder. He picked up the bottle, made sure the cap was tightly screwed on, then threw it over to me. I caught it and when I looked up again, he was gone. I heard his feet on the stairs and, a little bit later, the screen door slam.

Eventually, Sal pushed his chair back and stood up. I'm going out now, he said. When he got to the doorway, he turned around and said, When I get back, I don't want you to be here anymore. You understand me? I want you to leave.

I felt his words like arrows piercing my heart, but I didn't turn away. I just looked into his eyes and nodded. When he left the room, I started to cry.

I must have fallen asleep at the table because, when I woke up, the sky through the window was a faint metallic grey, the whole kitchen in black and white. I could hear a noise repeating itself and it took me a moment to realize that the phone was ringing. I sprang to my feet and hobbled stiffly down the hall. I picked up the receiver and said, hello. There was no answer and then finally a click and the line went dead.

I put the phone down slowly because suddenly I understood that it was time to move on. Time to leave again, and in a second I had made the break. I felt my heart seize up like a cramp, shut out all feeling, and rise like a stone into my mouth. I felt hard and blank. I walked back into the kitchen for my coat. I wanted to leave Jack a note or something. I got a pen and a piece of paper and my hand hovered for a while. I couldn't think of anything to say, so I put the pen down and was just about to leave when Kaleigh stepped into the kitchen. Her eyes were all puffy and red.

Who was it? she asked.

I dunno, I said.

Don't lie to me, John.

I'm not.

Was it Sal?

I told you, I don't know. There was no answer.

He didn't come home last night.

I know, I said, feeling more and more uneasy. I didn't want to get involved. I knew I couldn't stay and I didn't want Kaleigh to make it any more difficult for me than it already was. I had no sympathy left.

Oh, God, she said. I hope he's okay.

Okay? I said. What about me?

The door to Jack's bedroom opened and he shuffled out, came over and hugged Kaleigh's legs. He was still half asleep and Kaleigh picked him up and held him tightly in her arms. Whatever indifference I might have felt then did not include Jack and I wanted to tell him I loved him. I wanted to promise that I wouldn't let anybody hurt him, that no harm would ever come to him if only he could stay with me.

Kaleigh put her hand over Jack's ear and hugged him even closer. She was rocking him back and forth, her chin resting on the top of his curly head. She looked so vulnerable with Jack in her arms, determined to protect him from the world but unable to do so. Suddenly, the whole thing seemed so sad and pathetic. I had the urge to go over and take Jack away from her. I was sure I could do a better job. He needed someone strong. Someone who would fight for him. I took a step forward and Kaleigh moved backwards. Her eyes were wide and desperate. She looked frightened.

Are you afraid of me? I asked.

She didn't answer.

[249]

I wanted to take another step forward but something stopped me. I realized that it was too late, that everything had changed and there was no way things would ever go back to the way they were. I turned towards the door and left the kitchen. I walked mechanically down the stairs, one foot in front of the other. I felt like I was moving through mud, frozen mud. I propelled myself through the store and out the door. I got into my car, started the engine and pulled away from the Appleseed Emporium for the very last time.

Epilogue

In the window I see a reflection of a man in a dark grey sweatshirt. His eyes look deep and hollow in the shadow of his brow. His hair is thick and growing straight out the top of his head and he looks pale. It takes me a moment to recognize my own face.

I look down at the paper place-mat that is lying on the table in front of me. I'm holding a pen but don't remember having written anything. I have written my name across the top. Below it I have written, ANNA, in large block letters, dark from retracing. I've made a column of places: Bella Coola, Round Bay, Bridgewater. I bring my pen to the page again and draw an ⊢ in front of Anna's name. The letter is larger than anything else on the paper. It is hollow like a letter on a child's building block. I know where I am headed. For the first time in ages, I know where I am going. I add Montreal to the list of places.

I look out the window again. The white sky presses down like it wants to crush the earth. The parking lot is muddy and a yellow school bus pulls in. Teenagers in snowpants get off the bus and run over to the diner. I bring my hands up and run my fingers through my hair. I rub my eyes. I stare back at the bleak winter sky and all the pain comes flooding back to me.

I light another cigarette. The kids have come in from the

school bus. There's a rush of noise and the smell of wet wool and the double bang of downhill ski boots on the wooden floor. A pair of nylon pants swish past me towards the washroom. The kids are laughing and yelling at each other. A teacher corrals them into the far corner, near the pinball machines and the jukebox. A boy goes over and puts fifty cents in and presses a few buttons. He's about fifteen years old. I don't recognize the song but all the kids seem to know it. They mouth the words and a couple of boys jump up and start playing air guitar. It makes me feel old.

I stare at the children and there's a boy who could have been me four years ago, and a girl that looks like Anna, and one who could have been Babe, or Maureen, and I see a kid who could be Derrick and he's goofing around and teasing some girl. A whole new generation of the same types. Makes me feel we didn't have much say in the matter. Just history repeating itself.

The waitress comes over to refill my cup. You've been here for quite a while, she says. Everything alright?

Ya, I say and look at her pink frilly apron with the name of the diner written in black bubble letters. Rock Steady Eddies.

Rock on, I think to myself. Rock on.

They sure do make a helluva racket, these kids. School trips, she says. They come in every afternoon on weekdays and they're a drag to clean up after, let me tell you.

She stays where she is, leaning up against the booth as if she's waiting for me to pour out my soul. I don't want to give in to that uncanny telepathy that all waitresses possess. I resist it. They scare me. They're like high priestesses, taking confessions down on little pads. I feel vulnerable in their company and yet grateful, too. They have been my mothers and my sisters over the years. I seem to live in diners, but I'm tired of eating out. I want a home.

I sigh and get up. I thank the waitress and put my money down on the table. Outside, the air is cold and my jacket billows in the wind. I start the car and as it's warming I check the map. It's taken me a month to get this close and now I'm no more than twenty miles from the border. Suddenly, my stomach tightens and my heart begins to race. I'm not so sure I should do this anymore. I'm losing confidence. I lean my forehead against the steering wheel. I have no choice. I am being dragged like a hooked fish through the water. I leave the parking lot behind and drive on in silence.

It's not just Hannah but it's Canada that I'm returning to, like the prodigal son, hoping that it's absolution that is waiting for me and not the judgment of fathers. I'm anxious about the border crossing. It brings back memories of my childhood, of sleeping in motels and spending days on end in the car. I remember crossing the border with my dad. I remember his black eye, the way that hamburger made him wince. I can almost taste the salty rubber of my snorkel and feel the tight seal of my deep-sea diving mask.

I pull up to the booth and roll down my window. The border guard is French Canadian and talks in a heavy accent.

American? he asks me.

Yes, I say and pass him my license.

And where you going?

Montreal, I say.

How long?

Just a visit.

Yes, but for how long?

The weekend, I say, wondering if this will be true or whether, as I hope, I will plant down roots and grow old with Hannah.

I see, he says and inspects my driver's license. He looks over at a convex mirror to check my plates.

C'est beau, he says. *Continue*, and waves me clear across into the country of my birth and my heart is thumping out of control and the land is flat and barren and the trees to either side are weighted down with snow and between the trees the darkness deepens and draws me in. Occasionally, I pass another road or a house with its lights on because, by now, the sky is lead-grey and the blue snow gleams like icing over the fields. I have to turn the heat up full-blast to keep from shivering and I'm nervous because I'm in Canada now, and the whole place seems wild and mysterious to me.

After an hour or so, the country breaks and gives way to towns and suburbs. Finally, I approach the city. I can see the buildings in the distance, a cluster of skyscrapers, bright with electricity, shining like jewelled fingers, pointing the way downtown. A dark, flat hill is nestled in behind the buildings like a shoulder covered in dandruff. On the top is a cross lit up with white lights, holding its arms wide open to encompass the city.

I cross a bridge over a river with chunks of ice gripping the shoreline. The water is black and sinister. It's Friday evening and the streets are slow with traffic, snow piled high on either side. I don't know where to go, so I follow the car in front of me. I get behind a snow-plough grating along the street, shoving the slush and muck onto the sidewalk. A miniature plough follows it, tucking the snow neatly back along the gutter. Eventually, I find myself on a boulevard lined with shops and brasseries, Christmas decorations hanging from the street lamps.

I turn off into a side street and park a few blocks away. I lock the door and walk back towards the main road. There's a bar near the corner which I go into. The place is crowded with people speaking French. The air is hot and stifling. I order a beer and sit with my elbows on the bar and think about Hannah, what she's doing and what she looks like. I wonder if she's got a boyfriend. I imagine her face without the honey tan she picked up in California, winter-pale and fragile-looking, her lips more red, her hair almost black, but everything's so vague and I can barely remember what she looks like. I'm sure I'd recognize her in a crowd, instantly, from a distance, just from the way she moved or stood, but if I had to describe her features, for a police portrait for instance, I wouldn't be able to do it.

I take another swallow of beer then get up and walk over to a payphone by the bathrooms. I open the phone book and look up her name. There are half a dozen Crowes, but no H. Crowe, so I begin at the top and call the first number. A man answers but there's no Hannah there. The second number is busy, so I call the third. The line's been disconnected. The fourth and fifth also claim not to know a Hannah and I realize for the first time that it might be impossible to find her. Suddenly my decision to come here seems rash and desperate.

I push my way through the crowd and stand outside on the curb, breathless from the shock of the cold air. I tighten my collar around my neck and start walking. The sky above me is razor-sharp and the stars are humming like high-frequency radio signals. The air is static and subzero. I can see my breath as dense as smoke and my feet squeak on the hard-packed snow, the kind of noise the dentist makes when he's pushing the metallic filling down into the rotten core.

After walking for a few more blocks, I duck into another bar, quieter than the last and darker still. I stamp my feet on the wet carpet and find a seat in the corner at an empty table. A waitress comes over and changes my ashtray and asks me what I want to drink. A couple of minutes later she deposits a beer without a word and does so six more times over the next two hours and I am strangely gratified by the efficiency of this silent exchange. When I decide that it is time to go, I tip her well and stumble out into the night.

I head back in the direction I came from and turn down the now-deserted side street towards my car. I hear a whisper, like a sigh, and the snow on the branch of a pine tree shifts and falls to the ground like a sack of flour. The branch pops back up as weightless as a buoy and bobs up and down until there's no momentum left.

I no longer have any idea where I am going and none of my earlier conviction. I sit for a while with the engine idling until the car has warmed up, then drive along a road that leads up a hill. I stop at a lookout point and stare out at the bright grid of the city. There's nothing left for me here.

I continue driving until I find myself back on a bridge. It is the middle of the night and traffic is scarce. I slow down and look out across the river. There are blue chunks of ice floating on the black water. As I approach the middle of the bridge, I pull over and stop, stare out at the jagged edges of the St Lawrence, watch the slow progress of ice blocks along the shore, bumping into each other and breaking off, making the long journey down-river towards the Atlantic, and suddenly I yearn to be swallowed up by the water, dive into the current and be carried out to sea. Someone honks their horn as they drive by so I flick my hazards on. It's hot in the car and I lean my cheek against the cold glass.

I think about what it felt like as a boy to dive into the ocean, like I used to on nights like these, clear with a million stars overhead, when being alone was an adventure and I had my whole life in front of me and I wasn't afraid of the future. When I had hope and grace and guiltlessness. And now, nineteen years old, and all I feel is scared. Keep blaming myself for all the people who've ever abandoned me, as if I could have controlled the outcome. As if they would have stayed, still been alive if I had been a better boy. Like my mother.

I lean onto the steering wheel and feel the hot wet gush of tears.

I finally understand that it was never really about me, that it wasn't my fault and I don't know which is worse. It makes me feel alone in a whole new way. All I ever wanted was to feel connected, to be relieved of my own oppressive solitude, to know that I was good enough, special enough to have an effect on somebody else's life, even altered its course. I just wish someone cared enough that they couldn't live without me. But maybe that's too much to hope for. Maybe that will never happen. I need to get back to the root of things, accept the past and start from scratch.

There's a tap on the window. I turn to look and start winding the window down.

Excusez-moi, monsieur, a woman says. *Es-tu correcte?*

I don't speak French, I say, quickly wiping my face with the back of my hand.

Are you alright? she asks, switching into English.

I'm fine, I say.

And your car? It is okay?

Yes, thank you. It's fine. Just stopped to have a look.

I see, she says. I just thought . . . you see, I thought you might . . . she laughs, then grows serious and nods towards the river.

What, jump?

Yes, she says.

No, I'd never have the guts.

She looks at me for a moment as if to make sure, then says, Good.

I glance out over the water, then turn back to her and say, I'm very sorry.

Don't worry about it, she says, rubbing her arms and straightening up. It's very cold tonight.

Yes, it is.

Another car stops and a man gets out. Is everything alright? he asks, coming over.

Yes, I say, leaning out the window.

Just stopped to have a look, the woman says and waves towards the river.

Bit of a strange place for that, he says.

It's my fault, I say, and the man shrugs.

Cold night, isn't it, he says and the woman laughs again.

What's so funny? he asks.

That's what I just said.

Ah well, Canadians are obsessed with the weather, he says. That's all we ever talk about.

That's because we're at the mercy of the elements.

Specially on a night like this. Must be twenty-five below.

It's a hard time of year, the woman says quietly and looks up at the sky.

Sure is, he says, reaching into his parka and taking out a pack of cigarettes. He offers one to the woman and then to me. He lights our cigarettes and we smoke in silence. Another car slows down and the man waves it on.

Can you tell me how to get to the Trans-Canada Highway? I ask after a while.

Sure, the man says. You have to get off the bridge and turn around and come back this way. Then there are signs that you can follow.

Where are you going to go? the woman asks.

Bella Coola.

Where's that?

BC, I say. British Columbia.

But that's so far away, she says.

I know, but it's okay. It's where I'm from . . . It's my home.

I see, the woman says. Are you sure you're okay?

I'm fine now. Honestly.

Bon, bien, she says when she's finished her cigarette. She shivers and stomps her feet. *Joyeux Noël*.

Salut, the man says and shakes my hand.

I thank them and they head slowly back towards their cars.

They honk their horns and pull out into the middle lane. Merry Christmas! I call and wave as their tail-lights shrink into the distance.

I wind the window up, fasten my seat belt and put the car in gear.

Acknowledgements

I would like to thank Andrew Motion and Russell Celyn Jones for giving me confidence at a crucial stage, Jon Riley and Emma Platt at Faber and Faber for having faith in the book, and David Godwin for his enthusiasm and support, but especially for appreciating the art of artlessness.

And lastly, I would like to thank Richard Skinner, my tender critic.